ALSO BY LYNN MARGULIS AND DORION SAGAN

Microcosmos: Four Billion Years of Microbial Evolution

Origins of Sex: Three Billion Years of Genetic Recombination

Garden of Microbial Delights

MYSTERY DANCE

On the Evolution of Human Sexuality

Lynn Margulis and Dorion Sagan

SUMMIT BOOKS
New York • London • Toronto • Sydney • Tokyo • Singapore

 **SUMMIT BOOKS**
Simon & Schuster Building
Rockefeller Center
1230 Avenue of the Americas
New York, New York 10020

Library of Congress Cataloging in Publication Data

Margulis, Lynn, date.
    Mystery dance : on the evolution of human sexuality/
by Lynn Margulis, Dorion Sagan.
        p.   cm.
    Includes bibliographical references (p.   ) and index.
    1. Sex—History.   2. Sex (Biology)—History.
I. Sagan, Dorion, date.   II. Title.
    HQ12.M35   1991
    306.7′09—dc20   91-18450
                                                   CIP
ISBN 0-671-63341-4

Contents

Acknowledgments

We are deeply indebted to the numerous scientists, philosophers, and scholars without whose toil a book such as this would be neither fun nor possible. From before Aristotle and Plato through Samuel Butler and Charles Darwin in the last century to the indefatigable expanding cadre of sexual theorists in our own, we acknowledge the work of others. The panel participating in the symposium in New Orleans (American Association for the Advancement of Science) on "Sperm and Pollen Competition: The Importance of the Haploid" (Geoff Parker, Steven Austad, Jonathan Waage, David Mulcahy, and Robert L. Smith) offered a last-minute wave of insight, allowing us to put the finishing touches on the manuscript. We are grateful to Smith, whose thoroughgoing speculations on human sexual evolution filled in some of the crucial gaps in our story. For the sociocultural critique of evolutionary science, we are indebted to Donna Haraway, whose Summer 1990 session on primatologists at the Marine Biological Laboratory in Woods Hole questioned Darwinism, sexual selection theory, and male-oriented sociobiology in a most thoughtful way.

We are extremely grateful to Karen Nelson for expert and efficient manuscript preparation, and to our editor at Summit Books, Dominick Anfuso, for his hard, but ultimately effective criticism. We thank agents Katinka Matson and John Brockman for their usual encouragement and promotion of this manuscript, in all of its versions. David Abram, Peter Allport, J. Steven Alexander, Emil Ansarov, Charles Carroll, Eileen Crist, René Fester, Greg Hinkle,

Jennifer Klenz, Tom Lang, Mark McMenamin, Lorraine Olendzenski, Simon Robson, Robert and Stephanie Seber, Madeline Sunley, and Lynne Toland were among our friends who provided intellectual stimulation and aided in the innumerable small tasks required to complete the manuscript. Sisters Kristin and Kelly McKinney helped by lending a reference work and by diligently and enthusiastically reading some of the wilder, more deconstructive early drafts. Financial aid for the research came, if inadvertently, from the Richard Lounsbery Foundation (NYC), NASA Life Sciences, and the University of Massachusetts (Botany Department).

We would like to dedicate this book to all people who are struggling in relationships.

Introduction

EVOLUTIONARY
STRIPTEASE

Undress Rehearsal

Imagine a future in which three-dimensional holographic movies are shown, a future in which it is possible to recover DNA from fossils and "ghost" them—clone them, bring extinct beings back from the grave.

In such a future it would be possible to give a live presentation of what, in this book, remains purely a fantasy. The fantasy in question is that of a striptease. Not just any striptease, but an evolutionary striptease in which time present is put on rewind and our bodies are holographically unwound to reveal the salacious story of their sexual origins. In lieu of such a future—and because futures have the bad habit of never quite arriving—this book is set up as a kind of holographic theater, in which we show you evolution in reverse, from human to ape to reptile and beyond, exploring the evolution of men and women, sexual organs and sex roles, trusting commitments and erotic infidelities, love and lust.

Recent work by biologists has added much to our knowledge of sex. Drawing from philosophy and psychoanalysis as well as from rich scientific data this book tells a particular story of human sexuality. The "mystery dance" that unfolds on and between these pages is an imaginary striptease, a thought experiment that spotlights a phantasm called the evolutionary stripper, a kind of genetic genie whose undressing takes us far back in evolutionary time. The stripper's act exposes the presumed sex lives and bodily appearances of our ancestors, human and prehuman. The dancer, for example, takes off an outer layer of civilized monogamy to reveal the wanton promiscuity of *Homo erectus*, fire-using hunters ancestral to *Homo sapiens*. By sexually climaxing, *Homo erectus* females helped choose the genetic composition of modern humans. Beneath this layer—that is, earlier in time—lie the characteristic sexual features of human beings. The backward-moving steps of the mystery dance display the evolution of human sexual features such as prominent breasts, large penises and heavy testicles, the hymen, and the absence in females of estrus—of regular periods of sexual desire accompanied by vaginal swelling and pubic coloration.

The animal body evolves not only in response to external pressures of the environment but also to the sexual tastes of the opposite sex and in response to competition with other members of one's own. This book's evolutionary striptease shows how the primeval kinks, the likes and dislikes of our sexually arousable ancestors, molded the human body as it evolved from its apish predecessors. The stripper also reveals the biological foundations of overwhelming emotional states, such as raging sexual jealousy and self-destructive desire.

Physiologically the most important steps of our sexual history were undertaken by our remote predecessors. They occurred in epochs long before the appearance of the animal known as "man." Such paleobiological happenings, rarely described, include the origins of the penis, the reptilian "hieroglyphic" brain, and protist sexual cannibalism. Most ancient of all our living predecessors are those bacterial inhabitants of the sweltering early Earth from which all life has evolved. They are not sexless: bacteria already avidly exchanged genes—and therefore engaged in the planet's first sex—long before the existence of either plants or animals. Today the ancient ability of bacteria to offer and accept parts of themselves as genetic gifts in the formation of new, hybrid offspring is exploited in the laboratory, in biotechnology and genetic engineering.

The mystery dance is not exclusively the unveiling we call the evolutionary striptease; it is also the human sex act itself. From its obscure beginnings in the microcosm to the discovery of hormone birth control pills and mass production of rubber prophylactics, this mystery dance is our heritage. The slang word for coitus simultaneously means making love and an act of aggression. This duality is part of the secret of the mystery dance, an act that stands at the crossroads between the everyday and the transmundane, at that dusty fork where the vulgar meets the sacred, and reality hooks up with dream.

Shame

In 1584 women thought to be witches were being burned at the stake for committing "incestuous adulterie with spirits." A popular witch-hunting manual of the time asserted that the devil liked to assume the shape of a pretty wench and, in that form, seduce and make love to unsuspecting men. Keeping their semen the devil would then transmogrify into an incubus, a male sexual demon, and impregnate sleeping women as they dreamed. When Reginald Scot dared to publish that all this talk of men being "begotten without carnall copulation" was nonsense "speciallie to excuse and mainteine the knaveries and lecheries of idle priests and bawdie monkes; and to cover the shame of their lovers and concubines," King James of England ordered all copies of Scot's book burned.[1]*

We still dwell in a sexual dark age, although scientific discoveries concerning the roles of hormones, widespread avail-

---

*The Notes and References section begins on p. 207. It includes commentary on epigraphs, peripheral remarks, and other potentially disruptive statements parenthetical to the text.

ability of contraceptives that prevent pregnancy and venereal disease, and a more open, information-oriented society all indicate that sexual ignorance may be abating. It is true that women are no longer burned at the stake. But the prejudice toward homosexuals; the stridency surrounding the questions of sex education, abortion, and pornography; the difficulties of distinguishing healthy attitudes from subtle abuse and sex-ploitation—all these suggest that sexual enlightenment, if there is such a thing, has not yet arrived. In fact, the AIDS epidemic has had a dual effect: raising sexual consciousness and inspiring longer-term relationships on the one hand, and proliferating hypocritical moralizing and the scapegoating of gay men, Haitians, and intravenous drug users on the other.

Human sexuality resists the light of scientific inspection for several reasons. The widespread reticence and embarrassment that surrounds human sexuality result from its relation to those parts of the body that produce waste and over which our earliest job it was to exert control. *"Inter urinas et faeces nascimur,"* wrote St. Augustine: "Between piss and shit are we born." (Putting it vulgarly emphasizes the inhibition we feel in the face of this fact.) Toddlers are taught to control their bowels and urine; this is their first focus, their prime directive. In consequence, they despise their excrement, which they hide and which, psychoanalysis tells us, they associate with adult genitals and the fantasy of anal birth. The child as he or she is socialized learns that the bathroom, the bedroom, and certain parts of him- or herself demand privacy, entail mysteries; the sphincters must be covered and controlled. Surrounded by secrecy, the genitals are ridiculed, and the realms of childbirth, bodily evacuation, and sexual intercourse are confused. Misconceptions multiply.

Part of the problem with the relationship between the sexes later in life stems from the fact that we are, most of us, not only born of but reared by women. The central figure in the infantile life of both boys and girls is female—a mother who is loved and hated, who provides and denies, who coddles and neglects the baby before it is able to distinguish its five senses, differentiate inside from outside, or recognize itself or other human beings. As Dorothy Dinnerstein has shown in her book *The Mermaid and the Minotaur*, this early intense encounter with female humanity in the form of the mother has immense consequences: most of us in a dark corner of our mind continue to perceive woman from the prelogical vantage point of the infant, not as a human "she" but as an irrational "it," an abstraction as dangerous and indomitable as "nature" or "the flesh." Because of infantile experiences the body of the female remains magical, while the male tries to gain control over and access to that sort of body that was never sufficiently his own. What is male and human is defined in contrast to this early goddesslike power of the female. Dinnerstein suggests that men and women alike bear a lingering resentment against the woman because of the mother's power over us as infants, and that the only way to alleviate the culturally reinforced fear and hatred of women is for men to share equally in the raising of children. Dinnerstein's point is that the roots of sexual identity and feeling are buried in an infancy we have physically out-grown and "forgotten," but that this infancy continues to haunt us, producing negative adult attitudes toward women; alter-natively debased and exalted, worshipfully feared and resent-fully controlled, she is, like the mermaid, never really considered to be fully human.[2]

Another reason for the darkness surrounding sex may be its biological "depth": the sexual part of ourselves is so old, so deeply ingrained in our being as reproducing animal bodies that much of our sexual behavior is automatic, physiological, almost as deaf to our conscious wishes as the human heart, which beats regularly, naturally, as indeed it must if we are to live. In this sense sex is unconscious not because we have repressed its pain but because to be conscious of it would interfere with daily biological functioning. A final reason for the darkness surrounding sexuality is geographical: the West, unlike some Eastern countries, lacks a tradition of erotic spir-ituality. Western cultures have not integrated sexuality but marginalized it, kept it confined to the bedroom or on display as pornography, or used it to market wares. For the most part ours has been a tradition sanctioning sex within the family for the sake of childbearing, while reluctantly admitting the necessity of discreet prostitution and the existence of covert homosexuality. We Westerners have no Kama Sutra, no Tantra, no sacred sexuality. We do not publicly celebrate lesbian lovers or the passionate embraces of youths. Even today homosexuality is often still, as Oscar Wilde said of it in the last century, "the love that dare not speak its name."

Whatever its sociocultural expression, sexuality, intrinsic to human beings, reaches remotely back in time to a long line of nonhuman and inhuman ancestors. Beyond apes and past reptiles, amphibians, fish, and other vertebrates (animals with backbones), our sexuality descends from that of creatures who copulated and reproduced without anything resembling human form or behavior; this is why sex is no mere human phenomenon. We are indeed like mermaids and mermen in that we remain in touch with our former selves, a fleshy pastiche not just of fish but of thousands of ancestral lives. And if biology tells us that our body-minds embed their own ancient history, so too, psychoanalysis tells us that adult life is never completely released from the experiences of infancy and childhood. Sexual passions, fervent and confused, continue from a past we can ignore but not escape.

We begin to understand the sexual being of adult humans by tracing its hardly imaginable distant history. Fewer than one *million days* have passed since the birth of Christ; this book tells tales of bacterial beings living three *billion years* ago. The molecular, intracellular activities of these beings still exert a crucial influence on our sexuality. And so do the forms of our more familiar relatives. We jump forward prior to, shortly after, and during the appearance—according to the fossil record, four million years ago—of humanlike animals. Bones of australopithecines, *Australopithecus afarensis*, were unearthed near Hadar, Ethiopia. The males of some of these ancestors were nearly twice as large as the females: on our evolutionary lineage, physical domination by males and feminine submission may be ancient phenomena.

It is folly to ascribe human sexual behavior solely to biology, to immutable genes. Social Darwinists, politicians, and even

academics have used the idea of innate biological differences
to justify sexism and racism, causing feminists and liberals to
dismiss biology as "determinist." Biology, they claim, is "bio-
logistic"; by portraying the contingent historical knowledge of
our own culture as the immutable truths of all nature it provides the perfect excuse for maintaining an oppressive social
status quo. But although acutely aware of the potential for
erudite bigotry, we as a writer and a scientist nonetheless embrace evolutionary biology. Branding women as "inferior,"
some African races as "less evolved," or using such claims to
smugly pardon social inequalities as "natural" are all despi-
cable; such practices malign not only the scientist's case but
the case for science. Similarly, the claim that humans are so
genetically "programmed" that "instincts" are always impossible to transcend is ridiculous. But to reject evolutionary biology because of the excesses of its invokers is like throwing
away a pearl because it is surrounded by a strong-smelling,
seaweed-entangled oyster.

There is a strong case for the deep influence of our evolutionary history. The genetic potential for development is
inherited by all animals, including, of course, people. Many
behaviors are clearly genetic. All children, for example, sleep,
even in the womb. Intrauterine studies show that the unborn
have REM—rapid eye movements—just as dreamers do.
Sleep is not a learned or cultural trait: it is genetic (inherited)
and congenital (present at birth). All babies cry and reach for
the breast to suck. Children, on the average and compared
with adults, have a superior ability to learn a new language.
Although neither English nor Chinese are "built in" to the
genes, it is plausible to argue that the ability to babble and
then to speak is inherited and biologically timed such that
children learn to become members of their community, full-
fledged linguistic, human beings.

Nature and culture are far from clear-cut, independent categories; rather, they intertwine. Just as our bodies grow unconsciously within the womb and beyond the womb under
the choreographic powers of the genes, just as we breathe from
birth without the benefit of advice from doctor or "culture,"

so aspects of our sexual behavior are unlearned and inborn; they are "bred in the bone." And these are aspects, we believe, that are as embedded as they are unconscious, wielding great power over our lives as sexual beings. Far from dismissing those features as socially taught habits that can be unlearned, the best way to begin to outgrow them—if outgrow them we can—is to realize just how deeply—biologically—enmeshed in our being they are.

To what extent we can overcome the influence of the past is a problem in itself. An early reader of this book, Madeline Sunley, puts it eloquently: "One of my favorite questions about the future of our species is what I've come to think of as the horrified spectator question. Can we change destructive behaviors once we are aware of them? Or are we, at least at this stage of human evolution, trapped in a state of cognitive dissonance in which, powerless to change, we watch ourselves behave in ways we do not condone? This is one of the questions which lie at the very heart of a book like *Mystery Dance*."

Meaning and Being

It is easy to discuss human sexuality with clinical detachment, protected by a cloak of authorial objectivity or scientific expertise. But to talk of the mystery or meaning of sex is far more risky. Blanket statements verging on nonsense open a roomlike space in which sex can be seen for what it is. This book with its striptease invites a sense of voyeurism. In examining the human sexual experience, the reader sacrifices the security of "objective" knowledge to discover—and perhaps feel—more than he or she wants to know. Reading, you slide between the covers of a bedlike book as you confront these ink-stained sheets. Open eyes shift from side to side, just as they do during REM sleep. Indeed, in a sense this whole book is a kind of science "faction," a public, waking dream.

The French philosopher Jacques Derrida is the source of the intellectual ferment over "deconstruction." It is dangerous to define deconstruction, on the one hand because it has become such a loaded term, and on the other because its business has largely to do with subverting the conceptual, metaphysical categories policed by definitions. Deconstruction destabilizes texts—and ultimately the very notion of self-identity—by grafting them onto each other, unravelling weak arguments, and showing that authors often betray their own intentions. But Derrida has exploited the fact that the French word *lit* means both bed and read. Derrida playfully evokes this ever-present sexual underside of meaning even in the loftiest, most serious writings. For example, the English verb *mean* shares roots with *moan*, and we all know how quickly, once sought, sexual connotations surface. Even terms designating fields concerned with the study of meaning—such as *semantics* and *semiotics*—bear an evocative resemblance to the sexual word *semen*.[3] Such double entendres may seem distracting to the scientist but they are unavoidable. Moreover, they point beyond mere clinical sex research and the "facts" of biology to a compelling or compulsive study of the sexual depths of the human psyche.

According to the nineteenth century philosopher Friedrich Nietzsche, when women in ancient Greece tore apart and ate live chickens as they paid homage to Dionysus such homage to the god of wine evoked "above all the frenzy of sexual excitement, this most ancient and original form of frenzy".[4] The Dionysian pleasures of the feast, of *ecstasy* (literally: standing out of oneself), of conversation as psychosexual intercourse, of melding with or disappearing into the body of the other, of almost dying (a French expression for orgasm, *petit mort*, means "little death") . . . these are phenomenal experiences of sex that precede any high-handed scientific evaluation of human sexuality. A candid exploration of human sex leads to problems of meaning and being every bit as important and in some sense prior to the specific issue of the evolution of sex. Martin Heidegger, perhaps the most influential philosopher of the twentieth century, considers what has been translated as *Dasein*—"being there" or "human being"—along with *Sein*, "Being"—to be more primordial than any science such as psychology or biology. The study of being is called ontology. Some philosophers distinguish between the ontic—the realm of individual beings—and the ontological—"Being" in general. For Heidegger, both come before specific "derivative" sciences such as biology, psychology, and more broadly speaking, "technology," which although not a science like the others, is crucial for philosophy, according to Heidegger, since it defines the metaphysical character of our age. In addition to everything else, sexuality is ontic, part of our existence as living beings. And it may even be ontological, part of Being; to be alive is to experience a fundamental solitude, a loneliness that may be alleviated by the other, the lover, but never completely. This fundamental isolation of individuals from the universe Heidegger calls the "ontological difference." Sexuality comes into play because, however imperfectly, it provides a ready means of attempting to bridge this difference. Similarly, the mystical Eastern traditions suggest that individual personalities are only masks, and so, when lovers unite in sex, they may call forth a distinct state, in which the "I," the self, is seen to be an irresistible illusion.

The Stripper

The stripper in this book is androgynous. As (s)he takes off his/her clothes, we will be treated to views of our ancestors in earlier times. The stripper also is endowed with multiple identities. Sometimes (s)he will appear as a single person, a man or woman, sometimes as a mating couple, an animal, or a collection of microorganisms. The stripper, like the self in Eastern philosophy, has no discrete "I" but appears in all these guises. Each guise represents an evolutionary ancestor. Our working assumption is that virtually each of humanity's ancestors has left its mark, has helped mold human flesh and human nature in its ambiguity and complexity. Peeling off one layer presents us with views of the early human species, *Homo erectus* and prehuman lovers of the genus *Australo-*

pithecus (of which the famed "Lucy" skeleton is an example). We watch the changing stripper to find why apish females lost their body hair, pubic coloration, and developed permanently pendulous breasts. We learn that the woman's body itself is a form of practical feminism, deceiving males all too desirous of inseminating fertile females. And we find that the transfer from ape to human gave females greater control over their bodies, countering with cunning the superior physical strength of most males. But the ape in us, as important as it is, is only one guise, or disguise, in a striptease that brings us all the way back to our bacterial origins.

Peeling off another layer, the stripper exposes beneath the warm mammalian fur and the reassuringly familiar mammalian psyche, a cool level of "reptileness," including the "reptilian" brain—an ancient part of human anatomy shared not only with apes but with all mammals and reptiles. The R-complex, as the reptilian remnant of the human brain is sometimes called, remains. Overriding rational consciousness, this sex-attuned control center apparently undermines well-intentioned human beings, provoking reactions from jealous rage to impetuous abandonment and sudden passion. Modern reptiles lack keen hearing and an informative sense of smell; they *see* a patterned environment. Processing visual cues more with the retinas of their eyes than the cortex of their brains, reptiles communicate quickly, automatically, and by largely inborn means. Permanently "dumb," reptiles cannot learn to speak. Much of what we consider inhuman in ourselves may depend on an underlying reptilian sensibility, an archaic substratum that may suddenly and powerfully surface. Reptiles are dreamless, amoral slitherers who will kill on the spur of the moment but rarely form emotional attachments, even to their own egg-emerging offspring. It even seems that the mammalian ability to construct events into a chronological order occurred during the transition from the reptilian to the mammalian brain. Paradoxically, the sense of passing time itself evolved in these ancestors of ours. Dinosaurs and serpents—and our reptilian ancestors—cannot grasp stories. They appear to live in a permanent present, the waking reptilian equivalent

Geological Time Scale and Sexual Ancestors*

EON BEGAN	EONS	ERAS
0†	Phanerozoic	Cenozoic 66–0
		Mesozoic 245–66
		Paleozoic 580–245
580		
2,500	Proterozoic	
3,900	Archean	⎱ PrePhanerozoic
4,500	Hadean	

*Not to scale and simplified.
†Dates in millions of years ago.

PERIODS		EPOCHS		ANCESTORS
Neogene	26–0	Recent (Holocene)	0.1–now	Ape-people: *Homo sapiens*
		Pleistocene	2–0.1	*Homo erectus*
		Pleiocene	7–2	*Australopithecus*
		Miocene	26–7	
Paleogene	66–26	Oligocene	38–26	
		Eocene	54–38	
		Paleocene	66–54	First primates
Cretaceous	138–66			Age of
Jurassic	195–138			reptiles
Triassic	245–195			
Permian	290–245			Thecodont reptiles (dinosaurs and bird ancestors)
Carboniferous	345–290			
Devonian	400–345			
Silurian	440–400			Synapsids (mammallike reptiles)
Ordovician	500–440			
Cambrian	580–500			
				Protist mates
				Bacterial symbionts

to our nighttime dreamworld. But they can be moved by events and react quickly to a sign they perceive as a mate or threat.

Mammals and dinosaurs both evolved from an earlier group of so-called stem reptiles. Reconstructions from fossil bones reveal extinct ancestors, dog-toothed lizardlike beings and reptilian "weasels." Fossils of such mammallike reptiles abound on every continent but Antarctica. One paleontologist calculates that some 800 billion skeletons of mammallike reptiles exist in the Kaarroo beds of South Africa alone.[5] Evolving about 250 million years ago, populations of these creatures diversified prodigiously during the Permian and Triassic geological time periods (see Table).

The fossil record can be interpreted to mean that when the forerunners of the giant dinosaurs evolved—swift and vicious thecodonts—only a few mammallike reptiles survived. Unable to defend themselves against their increasingly brawny and ferocious cousins, the earliest mammals took to nightlife, hiding in the dark, in trees, and relocating to cooler climes, where they were free from molestation. These remote human ancestors, the mammallike reptiles or synapsids, were physically weaker than the thecodonts. Many fell prey to the fierce predators, but expanded sensory modalities—particularly the sense of hearing—evolved in those of our reptilian ancestors that survived. Cries, scratches, howls, and scurryings in their nocturnal dwellings warned skittish synapsids of the approach of aggressors and the retreat of potential prey. But in addition to these increased sensibilities, our four-legged forerunners retained the original deadly psychology of their reptilian heritage, their narrow focus on brute survival in the tropics: to kill, to avoid being eaten alive, and to copulate—these were the none-too-subtle means that had always ensured their reproduction. The foray into our reptilian ancestry, into the strangely familiar psychology of reptiles, brings us into contact with psychology. And its most radical offshoot, psychoanalysis.

Freud's French follower, Jacques Lacan, insists upon the absolute central importance of the phallus as a symbol or signifier—not so much for the penis as for what is missing—a lack-in-being (*manque-à-être*) or castration at the heart of all would-be communication. The phallus is an erotic arrow pointing beyond the confines of evolutionary biology into the dark continent of psychoanalysis. It leads us from a discussion of the evolution of the penis back again to familiar territory whence humanity came. Although we are by no means completely convinced by them, we stop to discuss theories of the phallic signifier, the mirror stage, and the infant's magical psyche as the evolutionary dance continues and the striptease recedes further into the womb of time.

The large average size of the human penis (five to six inches, versus three for chimps, and one-half that for gorillas) may have been, evolutionists speculate, to frighten other males. Or to attract females. Or to enhance their pleasure. Perhaps the best hypothesis is that the longer penis delivers sperm more closely to the eggs: today's biologists claim that for females who mated with several males, the male with the longest penis delivered his sperm more safely. The first penislike organs probably arose in fish or amphibians whose ancestors had reproduced solely by external fertilization, by spawning outside bodies, in the warm water of lakes or the frothy ocean. The warmth and wetness of the human sex act recalls the breeding grounds—water—of those amphibians and fish ancestral to reptiles. As the mystery dance continues, our lizardlike forerunners disappear. These were disseminators of sperm who competed for females without benefit even of a penis and shook the muddy water off their smooth and shiny bodies before slinking on.

Before our amphibious ancestry and beneath the stripper's amphibious dress lie the soft-bodied animals sometimes called Ediacaran fauna after the place where they were first found. But these strange gelatinous beings are rarely preserved in the rock record and may not contain any of our direct antecedents. And if quivering jellyfishlike animals are difficult to find, the colonial microorganisms that preceded them are still more elusive.

Wet and slippery, sex does not fossilize well. Unlike trilobite animals languishing on ancient seashores, insects trapped in sticky plant resin before it becomes amber, or ape lovers dragging their feet and thereby leaving footprints in a romantic stroll through drying mud, the microscopic events at the heart of sex are rarely preserved in the rock record. Life is thought to have begun as oily molecules formed in tide pools of warm shallow seas; the first life, bacterial slime, spread as a kind of briny, colorful mucus—the slippery "microbial mats" or hard domes called stromatolites that still today in remote places such as Western Australia creep inexorably toward the sunlit surf. In both a physical and metaphysical sense, human sexual activity returns the body to the softness of its marine origins, to a time when life had not yet hardened, protected, and extended itself by incorporating durable substances such as lignin, shell, and bone. The engorged, the damp and brackish genitals engender the warm environment of ancient genes. They re-present a past present when single-celled beings looking much like sperm and ova existed but the human bodies that now produce them did not. It is among these cells—protists—that look so much like free-living sperm or egg cells that some of our most remote ancestors are to be found.

The mysterious and highly varied sex lives of protists hold secrets and clues for a comprehensive understanding of human sex. Yet even before the protists, the bacterial progenitors of all life lived on Earth. Some of the oldest unmetamorphosed rocks on Earth bear witness to ancient bacteria caught in the act of dividing. In Swaziland in southeast Africa are sedimentary rocks that, cut into thin strips and viewed under the high-power light microscope, reveal fossilized fission, the most simple means of reproduction known. But such bacterial fission is virtually the opposite of sex, of fertilization, of cell fusion: it is reproduction in the absence of sex. No fossil yet found preserves protist cell division, the process called mitosis that makes two perfect copies of the parent cell. And certainly no meiosis—truly sexual cell division making sperm or eggs with only half the parental number of chromosomes—has ever been found preserved in the fossil record. Yet fossil flower parts and petrified egg shells attest to the ancient history of meiotic sex. It is because of this second cell division process, meiosis, that animals like us must seek out and join up with the opposite sex to make a new fused, or fertilized, cell, a cell that squares the circle, makes the half a whole again. Meiosis has long been a cellular imperative: genes that survived into the next generation depended on the meiotic production of egg cells and sperm and their fusing within the female's fallopian tubes.

Since meiotic sexuality is present in some protists, absent in others, and represented in a sort of half-hewn or midway state in still others, it seems likely that the kind of sexuality and cell fusion that brings man-sperm and woman-egg together began in watery protists, most of which are invisible to the unaided eye. The question is, how did protists—these microbes, more complex than the bacteria but less complex than the first animals—ever hit upon the trick of fertilization: doubling up their nuclei, chromosomes, and genes once each generation? And what is the point of this doubling, when the doubled cell only splits up again by meiosis to form sperm and egg? "One routinely recites the horrors of sex, metabolic, venereal, and behavioral, with the inevitable punch line, 'And for all your troubles your children carry only half your genes,' " writes University of Virginia biologist Robert Kretsinger.[6] Although Kretsinger suggests this paradox is used mainly to titillate students despondent about grueling exams, evolutionary biologists have, in fact, debated it at great length. The potential answers are complex but often revolve around the idea that meiotic sexuality must confer some great benefit—for example, that it must somehow "speed up" evolution, or have some other function that keeps it from disappearing. Scientists have reached no consensus. The actions in the evolutionary striptease, however, underscore our idea that meiotic sex, in and of itself, may have no clear evolutionary reason or purpose. Our tiny ancestors simply got caught in a ritual dance, now beyond mere habit, of cannibalism, cellular fusion, and partial regurgitation. Without immune systems, it was possible for our microbial ancestors to swallow each other whole, digest only part of the meal, and extrude the living rest. Like many a distasteful survival story it sounds disgusting, but this first meiotic sex worked: those beings that took the bitter pill of protist cannibalism persisted; they lived to pass on their genes.

Microbial sex—meiosis and fertilization—has cast a long shadow over the existence of animals. While all-female species of lizards and rotifers reproduce parthenogenetically—without benefit of males ever—even they retain unmistakable traces of the cellular dance of meiosis. The peculiar sex lives of protists linger on, and the protists at least go through the motions of the billion-year-old events crucial to their reproduction, if not feverishly and faithfully replaying them with no loss of original ardor.

No person today dispenses with the return every generation to "germ" cells. The eggs that menstruating women shed and the sperm that men ejaculate each have only a single set of chromosomes. Until their fateful meeting inside the woman— an old saying states that life begins and ends at the back walls of the vagina—the sperm and ovum each still possess only one single set of chromosomes. All people—embryos, fetuses, babies, children, and adults—absolutely require two complete sets of chromosomes to live. More than any body part, these chromosomally stripped cells, squirming sperm and sticky ova, resemble our free-living protist ancestors. Ensuring their doubleness, the microbeasts became stuck in the original sexual relationship, a slippery routine of merging and emerging, smothering and removal, bondage and escape. They live on deep inside us.

But sexuality started much earlier than the cannibalistic gorging cells with nuclei that engulfed each other during times of drought and starvation. Sex began on a planet whose only inhabitants were the colorful, promiscuous bacteria, tiny, colonial beings incessantly exchanging their genes. Sex began during the Archean eon on a planet with an atmosphere very different from that of today. This planet was zapped by lightning and scorched relentlessly by ultraviolet radiation from the sun. As the evolutionary stripper will show us, bacterial promiscuity most likely arose from chemical mechanisms of DNA repair that evolved in cells damaged by solar radiation.

Bacterial sexuality differs fundamentally from the sexuality of organisms with nuclei (protists, plants, fungi, and animals), in that it occurs independently of reproduction, crosses "species" barriers, and involves, in principle, the sexual sharing of genes by bacteria all over the world. Indeed, Canadian bacteriologist Sorin Sonea points out that bacteria, since they are able to trade genes freely across would-be species barriers, are not really assignable to species at all. In nature, bacteria with their uncounted numbers and metabolic types form a global "superorganism" whose bodily contours are those of the biosphere itself. This superorganism is unequivocally "sexual": it is continually trading genes among its myriad parts. It literally has sex with itself. Although sex in bacteria does not lead to single offspring with two parents, as it does in reproducing mammals, sex in the microcosm leads to genetic novelty. The global community of bacteria, which accounts for the transport of carbon, nitrogen, and all other biogeochemical cycles of the biosphere, is nearly four billion years old. Such age is almost inconceivable, verging on immortality. To this age-old superorganism the entire odyssey of humanity from shaggy erect ape to computerized corporation would appear no more substantial than the passing fancy of a butterfly. Indeed, compared to the solid tenure on this Earth of the bacteria-run biospheric superorganism, the stay of *Homo sapiens* is a mere blip.

It might seem that the microbial phase is the stripper's last, when (s)he loses everything and the dance is done. But there is perhaps a still deeper phase, the metaphysical plane of pure phenomena, continuous appearances. The evolutionary stripper is a curious creature: the G-string is not a thin cloth decorated with tassels but rather a word, a letter, a musical symbol for ultimate nakedness. Paradoxically, when the G-string is removed—to the accompaniment of strange vibratory music, consisting in part of a silent triangle and a gentle crash of cymbals—the nakedness itself is gone. S(he) stands before us as fully dressed as ever before.

At first glance, with the genetic exchange in bacteria, the most elemental living beings, it appears that we have reached the end of the evolutionary striptease, reduced sexuality to its essence. But no: there is always more. Not only the nature but even the possibility of any final revelation is in doubt. The whole masquerade of the evolutionary striptease depends throughout upon a type of information completely different from molecular biology's genes but no less essential: phonemes, graphemes—words. We encounter our sexual ancestors along the slippery slope of signs and signifiers, via the medium of language. The use of signs of any kind necessarily obscures; words represent or replace signified things in absentia; they are little black masks. We postpone reality to discuss it; without this postponement, this instantaneous replacement of our sexual ancestors, or things in general, by their signs there could be no possibility of language, of signification at all. Language is dead material: a burnt stick, a sliver of bark, substitution for the living presence. But it is not only the little black marks of the alphabet that stand in the stead of real things, or at least of real sounds: the whole world is at a remove from itself. There is no simple purity of presence.

Jacques Derrida claims the idea that there is any presence to start with, that there is, as Gertrude Stein might say, any "there there," is itself in question. The idea of presence, a metaphysical construct, is not limited to writing, but is applicable to writing in the wider sense given it by Derrida. "There is no outside-text," writes Derrida.[7] This means: nothing simple existed freely at the origin that unambiguously gave rise to complexity, obscurity, and impurity. Complexity, obscurity, and veiling are always already with us. Such thoughts are important for our idea of knowledge through discovery because they suggest that despite the continuous unveiling the evolutionary striptease conceals as much as it reveals. Truth cannot return to a revealing nakedness it never had.

Jean-Jacques Rousseau longed for the innocence of his unspoiled youth, the fresh smells of the countryside, and the dancing of children. Derrida describing this in *Of Grammatology* contrasts Rousseau's idea of an original innocence and plenitude with the feelings of loss—of loss of "presence"—to which Rousseau guiltily confesses in descriptions of "conjuring forth absent beauties" while masturbating. Rousseau, as Derrida shows, yearns in vain. At the origin the presence is not a presence; it is already the memory of a presence. The evolutionary dancer, the exotic chronicler of our sexual past slides out of personhood again and again in the frenzied attempt to show us the truth of our origins. But (s)he cannot. Instead of the past being disclosed, we confront an idea of the past in the present. (S)he is fickle. Now (s)he shows up as the scientific truth of our past, now as a naked metaphor: a paper dress patterned with these very words.

We are almost ready to enter the imaginary theater, dim the lights, and watch the holographic machinations of the evolutionary stripper as (s)he begins undressing. But first a brief note on time.

Time

Most people think of time simply as a passing stream of "nows" in which what has passed away is in the past, whereas what is future has still to come. We speak of "water under the bridge" and the "flow" of time. But this common image of time as a stream may be largely due to language. Indeed, some linguists believe that speaking different languages coincides not merely with different words but with distinct ways of thinking, of ordering and perceiving the world. If true, then language directs our view of time. For example, occasionally we speak of what's "around the corner" or "over the horizon"—seeing our future as a place blocked to vision, but generally the language leads us, as English-speakers, to think that our past is *behind* us. A different "past," by contrast, has been attributed to native speakers of the Navajo language. History, in the spatial metaphor of the Navajo language, is *in front of you*.[8] This makes sense: we can see where we have been; it is the future, not the past that remains opaque, impossible to see.

The Navajos back into the future with the panorama of the past before them—as if life were a train ride in which the passenger faces the rear. Keeping in mind this "new" Navajo view of time, we turn our mind's eye to the stage, where the past is clearly laid out ahead of us—far more clearly than the future at our backs.

I

SPERM
CONTEST

I would love to kiss you
The price of kissing is your life

Now my loving is running toward my life shouting
What a bargain, let's buy it

—RUMI (1296)

As the stripper peels off the first layer, we see that beneath our humanity lie apelike beings, and that the bodies of modern men attest to promiscuity in our apish ancestors.

The spotlight falls, the curtains part, and the show begins. Through a mist we see a young woman. Unwrapping the scarf from her face reveals black lipstick on her lips, blue glitter on her eyelids, and rouge on her cheeks. She slides out of her clothes to music, appearing naked before us. She slowly turns, now exposing the broad muscular shoulders of a baseball pitcher. Poised for the overhand aim, as he snaps into focus his right arm holds a poisoned spear. His nostrils flare, his penis flaccid. The stripper is at once a father and a son. Alleviator of tribal hunger, he is the man who returned full-handed from the hunt. The accurate, visually acute human predator who, if he were

*unable to concentrate on the hunt, became the tiger's prey.
This exotic dance is just beginning. With a pirouette, the evolutionary stripper reveals that this human body is itself a
garment. The broad-chested, slender-hipped figure dissolves
amid hallucinatory beams of colored light. A paleolithic person
emerges, topless, a moist grass skirt adorning her hips. Her face
is streaked with cosmetics of colored clay. Although small and
lithe, she is an adult woman who disappears as her grass skirt
dissolves into flesh and a larger estrous apewoman shows up.
She has a sloping forehead, large jaw, flat chest, thin hips, and
a prominent brow. Although this large female is too hairy and
stooped to appeal sexually to a contemporary man, the sight
of her might stir his imagination. The apewoman's teeth are
bared as she turns to show her swollen vulva. As she turns
again, her buttocks, decorated in shades of mauve and purplish
pink, jut out. Growing still larger, more hairy, "she" is now
become male. His pointed canine teeth protrude as his scrotum
contracts. His ape genitals are far less conspicuous than his big
body, long arms, and huge, crooked toes. With brown, wet hair
and eyes, exuding animal odors into the holographic theater,
this grunting ape-man sniffs the air. He rudely probes the bushy
tangle of his smaller species-mate for the pinkish mauve he
craves. Embracing, the two shrink into one eerily familiar primate, with chimplike face and hair-covered gorilla-shaped skull.
The intelligence shining from the eyes of this creature is still
surprisingly human.*

The Genital Record

The average length of the erect penis of a man is
some five times that of an adult gorilla. Human testicles, which
hang down, are also considerably larger than those of gorillas
and orangutans, two of our closest genetic relatives. This scan-
dal of comparative anatomy—the relatively gigantic genitalia
of human males—provides circumstantial evidence about the
sex lives of some of our early human ancestors.

Large testes and big penises are advantages only under conditions of widespread sexual promiscuity. Among our closest relatives the great apes, only male chimpanzees have testicles more prodigious than those of men. And chimps, with their big, heavy testicles, are more sexually promiscuous than humans. That the sperm-producing organs of chimps and humans are relatively big and heavy strongly suggests that some of our not-so-distant hominoid ancestors were far more promiscuous than gorillas or orangutans—or than many people are today. In the evolutionary past, the competition to reach primate eggs was sometimes between sperm from different male donors. If two or more males copulated with the same female within a period of days, an advantage in begetting offspring accrued to the one who ejaculated the greatest quantity of vigorous sperm cells. Like an auto race won by the driver whose sponsoring company can afford to provide him with the most souped-up car, the male with the best-timed copulation, most far-reaching ejaculation, and biggest testicular "engine" able to produce the greatest quantity of sperm tended to win the "game" of impregnation. Souped-up genitals with a lot of spermatic firepower, like incredibly expensive streamlined racing cars, are worth it only if there is some sort of race or contest. Otherwise they seem excessive.

If nature had a sense of morals we could accuse it of being depraved, but it doesn't, so we can't. Milan Kundera in his story *The Farewell Party* describes a wily, large-nosed obstetrician who treats barren married women through the questionable expedient of artificially inseminating them with his own virile sperm. Professionally execrable, and certainly no great lover in the usual sense, Kundera's doctor is nonetheless a genetic winner, fathering the (large-nosed) children of several happy although cuckolded husbands. So, too, the orb-weaver spider eats her mate alive as he copulates with her. In predatory insects known as mecopterans, the male has to regurgitate "foam balls" or capture edible prey for the females, who choose their sex partners on the basis of who provides them with the most succulent gifts. In one species of mites the brother inseminates his sisters and dies while still inside the mother, whose nutritious body is eaten to death inside out by the incestuous females, all of which are born pregnant. The kamikaze honeybee drone's genitals, sporting yellowish horns and an assortment of flanges and bristles, burst forth at sexual climax in the queen like a spring trap, forming a natural chastity belt barring entrance to other suitors even as the drone plops to the ground and dies. The Marquis de Sade is said to have carried with him a pillbox full of candy-coated Spanish fly, which he would offer to unsuspecting prostitutes; the Spanish fly, an "aphrodisiac" that works by irritating the urogenital tract, induces copulation in animals, including, presumably, humans. What we learn from looking at such "perversity" is that even the most normal, socially acceptable modes of human sexual behavior are not universal but particular variations on the general theme of animal survival. As species change, their standards change. Evolution itself has no master morality, and the most objectionable tactics often succeed best.

Throughout the animal world the relationship between the sexes is a kind of flowery combat, fought with sex scents and promises, full of slick deceits and unconscious intrigue, treacherous, with occasional truces, ending up as often as not in ignorance or disillusion after achieving the needed genetic agenda, the evolutionary mission of producing offspring. In all sexually reproducing species, males and females depend upon each other's bodies to deliver their genes into the next generations. Apart from passionate physical union in the sexual act, there may be little contact between them. No evolutionary mandate requires the sexes to be either civil to or inconsiderate of each other. From a general biological standpoint, possessiveness, elopement, marriage, castration, the desire of lovers to "be alone together" are as aberrant as the inferred promiscuity of our ancestors—they are the sexual idiosyncrasies, the often unconscious survival techniques, of the human animal.

The evolution of large human genitalia under past conditions of promiscuity is an example of what Charles Darwin called sexual selection. Darwin invoked sexual selection to explain the appearance of animal bodily traits that did not make sense to him in terms of the struggle for existence or natural selection. Darwin saw sexual selection acting in two main ways: (1) between the sexes, for example, as ancestral human females chose males with attractive patterns of facial hair and (2) within a sex, for example, as semihuman males wrestled each other for possession of young females. The traits that would be selected by these processes—in this case beards and muscles—would arise not from the general struggle to survive but from the special problems of sexual beings that need to find mates to reproduce.

As Charles Darwin recognized, competition between the males of a species for access to females leads to the evolution of exotic attributes such as the antlers of caribou who lock their horns—sometimes to the death—in rutting season. But this sort of brutal vying between males for entry to the bodies of females—one of Darwin's two main types of sexual selection—is not the only sort of male competition. We now know that the erotic prehistory of humanity is bawdier than was thought. We know about sperm competition from new evolutionary work that compares animal mating, anatomies, and behaviors. Whenever a female mates with more than one male during a single reproductive cycle, millions of sperm from two or more ejaculates swim toward their goal: fertilization of the relatively scarce ova. Multimatings start a round of sperm competition. And sperm competitors need not be dangerous brutes or wide bodies. They just must have the equipment to fertilize females who mate with more than a single male.

Sperm Competition

Sexual theorists, in analyzing the animal or "diploid" phase of a life cycle, tend to ignore the haploid sperm. Diploid refers to the presence of two sets of chromosomes; all the cells of an adult mammal are diploid except the sperm or egg cells. With only one set of chromosomes, these latter reproductive cells are "haploid." Not until Geoff A. Parker, a

zoologist at the University of Liverpool, England, elucidated
the concept of sperm competition in papers he wrote during
the 1970s, was it realized to what extent sexual selection occurs
in the haploid phase, that is to say, at the level of eggs and
sperm. Darwin, although he had his Victorian scruples, certainly speculated boldly on sexuality. One cannot accuse him
of being a prude, for he wrote about the "hinder ends" of
monkeys and the cumulative effects of sexual choice in early
human tribes. But, perhaps because he knew little of life on
the microscopic scale of cells, Darwin never discussed sperm
competition or its role in forming the bodies of men. He may
simply have overlooked the evidence of comparative ape genitalia in his musings on the "descent of man."

In monkeys and apes, variations in testes size seem to reflect
a striking difference in primate breeding systems, in, that is,
the socially acceptable level of promiscuity. Chimpanzees have
a kind of "free sex" breeding system wherein a female in heat
will mate often and in succession with many adult males,
whereas gorillas are "harem" apes in which one male watches
possessively over the sexual activity of several females. In species where female promiscuity is pronounced, male testes are
relatively prodigious sperm producers: while male chimps (Pan
troglodytes) are about one-quarter the weight of male gorillas
(Gorilla gorilla), their testes are some four times heavier. Test-
ing Parker's seminal ideas in mammals, the English biologists
Paul H. Harvey and A. H. Harcourt have concluded that
"comparative data on body size, testes size, and breeding system confirm the prediction that multi-male primates have large
testes for their body size."[1]

For their part, the males of some chimpanzees tend to sexually share rather than vigilantly guard females. Adolescent
females leave their natal groups to enter other groups whose
males, but not females, are closely related to each other.
Troops of chimpanzees composed of genetically related males
typically hunt, and sometimes kill, less related male chimps.
This sort of "male bonding" extends to the willingness of such
chimps to permit other males in the troop to engage in sexual
intercourse with a female in heat, one from outside the troop.

This less possessive sort of mating has detectable evolutionary consequences. Rampant female mating leads to competition not before but after copulation, and not among bodies but among sperm. A female copulates with several males whose sperm compete to fertilize her. Sperm competition can occur even if a female copulates with different males several days apart. This is because sperm are hardy and may survive in the vagina of a chimpanzee or woman for as long as eight or nine days.

Any female who copulates with more than a single male while ovulating opens the gates to a sperm race. The males or men who produce the sperm are not direct entrants; they are more like the corporate sponsors advertising their name and providing financial backing. Not all participants in the all-male marathon are equally prepared to win. Mammals who mate more frequently, and produce more sperm per ejaculation, are more likely to impregnate their partners.

Favoring the sperm of one male over that of competitors are such things as position during sexual intercourse, force and timing of pelvic thrusting, number and speed of ejaculated sperm, and proximity of the spermatic means of delivery—the penis—to the egg at time of ejaculation. Copious sperm production (estimated by testicle weight), deep penetration, and an elongated penis are all presumably advantages to males engaged in sperm competition. Perhaps most important is sheer sexual vigor, with more active males ejaculating the greatest number of times gaining a competitive edge. The charm and proficiency of a male—his ability to seduce a female and to continue to please after seducing her—of course also crucially determine his chances of entering and therefore of winning the competition; and in this sense females make the great impact of generally deciding who will and will not compete. There is also evidence that a woman who climaxes while making love to her lover is more likely to become pregnant by him.

So after Darwin we have learned that male competition may be "peaceful" as well as brutal, leading to male "tools" effective not in killing but in loving. The copious sperm producer, the male with heavy testicles and long erection capable of powerful ejaculation into the depths of the vagina places his sperm before that of others, or displaces previously deposited sperm. He tends to beget sons with similar anatomical endowments.

But the legacy of sperm competition is not confined to men's anatomies. The need to compete in the sperm contest has also had detectable effects on human male physiology and psychology. Laboratory tests, for example, have been recently done in Manchester, England that show that men who know or are suspicious of the promiscuity of their mates tend to load their testes with extra sperm. To make the tests, sperm counts are taken after grading a man as to his confidence in or suspicion of the fidelity of his wife or lover. Men who suspect their mates are cheating produce more sperm cells and more semen per ejaculation than they do when they trust in their mates' fidelity; titillated by sexual suspicion, their bodies adjust, try to maintain dominant reproductive access by usurping the woman's reproductive tract and supplanting a second male's sperm. Presumably, this loading of the testes acted in evolutionary time as a rationing mechanism, allowing the body to conserve its resources, economize on biochemicals that can also be used to produce fertile semen. When the paired female seems faithful, the male body saves itself. When she seems unfaithful, it goes to work overtime. Jealousy is an aphrodisiac. This unconscious control of sperm production is certainly evidence for the existence of sperm competition in humans. [2]

Further graphic evidence involves a German woman who bore twins, one of whom was mulatto—the son of an American serviceman—and the other who was a white son of a German businessman. In this case, the fathers "tied" in the sperm race. The woman produced two eggs, and two ethnically distinct children resulted. [3]

The number of sperm cells released in a single ejaculation of one man is 175 thousand times more than the number of eggs a woman produces in her entire lifetime. It can be more than the number of people in North America: hundreds of millions. Sperm are rapidly produced and expendable, whereas eggs are rare and precious. Since the growth of the embryo took place in women's wombs, nonnegotiably committing them to at least nine months of gestation and often a year or more of breast-feeding, it is no wonder that women have become somewhat more reluctant than men to copulate. Apart from risks of death during childbirth, the helpless human infant requires such attention that, without birth control, human mothers were more successful if they postponed sexual intercourse until they could be relatively sure their children would be well cared for. The caution must have been especially true of the past, before birth control permitted women to engage in sex for pleasure without pregnancy worries. One of the main conclusions Charles Darwin derived from his observations of the sexual habits of animals was that the females of many species tend to be "coy," choosing males rather than being chosen by them. Darwin, like other Victorian scientists, was a male chauvinist; he hedged his comments on the active role of females in evolution by suggesting that females "chose" males who had already defeated their competitors in male–male combat—not a real choice at all but a Hobson's choice, similar to a magician forcing a card. Darwin thus undermined his insight of the female role in evolution by stopping short of attributing to females full power to have molded the seemingly decorative features of many male animals from plumage of birds to the sagittal crest on the head of the male gorilla.

Darwin, impressed by the colorful plumage of male birds and the bright painted-looking faces and buttocks of some monkeys, theorized that such markings had evolved because they were attractive to females. Females, Darwin pessimistically put it, pair with "the least distasteful males." In these days of punk mohawks and purple hair it is also interesting to note that some scientists now attribute some of the most eccentric traits of the dinosaurs—such as the three horns of the *Triceratops*, and the backward-pointing head handle of *Parasaurolophus*—to female choice. But male charm and fighting ability most impressed Darwin; he reckoned male battles were caused by a perpetual scarcity of potential mothers.

Darwin was probably protecting himself from the accusation that he was implying that male animals evolved according to female caprice or whim; it is clear that he doubted his readers would believe in the aesthetic powers he was arguing were possessed by female animals. So, on the one hand, Darwin proposed the grand idea that the mane of the lion and the plumage of the peacock may be the result of the tastes of female animals, while, on the other hand, he held that female animals were not that important in evolution but will be, as his grandfather Erasmus had written, "observed like the ladies in the times of chivalry, to attend the care of the victor."[4]

Darwin could have been bolder in his speculations on female choice. Recent studies tend to confirm that females show much sexual initiative, and will even reject aggressive males as mates despite their fighting ability. One study of Japanese macaques reports that some of the females chose to consort with other females, although there was no lack of courting mature males. Since the females of many species perform the greater part of nurturing, and since male sperm is rarely a scarce commodity, females appear to be doing far more in evolution than blindly accepting the winners of male–male struggles.

The importance of the female role in evolution extends to the subvisible realm of sperm cells themselves. Biologist Steve Austad of Harvard University has studied sexual selection in flour beetles and European spiders; Austad believes that females may play an active role in deciding which sperm will fertilize their eggs even when they harbor the sperm of more than one male inside them. Austad prefers the term "sperm precedence" over "sperm competition," since the latter implies that the female has no control. He found in his experiments with genetically marked European spiders that the earliest male to mate does not necessarily gain an advantage in fertilizing a female. In these spiders, females only mate while they are eating a gift of prey the male has offered them. Ruling out statistical error, Austad showed that successful fertilization is correlated with mating duration—which could be related to female preference.[5] Certain spiders, in other words, may mate longer with the males they like, helping to choose the sperm that will fertilize them. It does indeed seem that even "sperm competition" is not an affair simply among males but that some females may deeply influence paternity.

Although females can deeply influence paternity, part of the dialectic of the sexes is that males stand to gain from circumventing that influence. Males are compelled to find ways to fertilize their females—often regardless of female preference. Sperm of both the octopus and the dogfish shark is packed with serotonin—a simple compound related to the ubiquitous amino acid tryptophan. Serotonin transmits nerve impulses, acts as a muscle stimulant, and cunningly induces powerful uterine contractions. Serotonin thus effectively short-circuits any female choice after copulation; it elicits an unconscious physiological response. Zapped by serotonin, the uterus contracts, "swallowing" the sperm.

Even human semen contains chemical compounds that function like those of the dogfish shark. A man's semen is ejaculated in fluids produced by the seminal vesicles, Cowper's glands, and the prostate. The alkalinity of these fluids buffers the sperm, protecting it against the acidity of the vaginal environment. But the seminal fluids also contain prostaglandins. Recent research indicates that prostaglandins are associated in women with pleasurable uterine contractions—contractions that pull the sperm toward their destination. And yet males do not necessarily have the last word, since other recent research indicates that female orgasm, over which women have primary control, also creates intrauterine suction capable of "spotting" the sperm of one man an advantage over that of another.

The obligation to engage in sex to reproduce helps explain why people will put themselves in dangerous situations and risk their lives and livelihoods in order to gain the opportunity of sexual pleasure or romantic adventure. Romantic foolishness makes evolutionary sense because it is the genes in the nucleus of the sperm and in the nucleus and mitochondria of the ova that survive in evolutionary time; men and women, by contrast, always die. It makes little difference what happens to the bodies housing the immortal genes in sex cells after these bodies reproduce. In contemporary biology the "phenotype"—the body—is often thought of as an ingenious but disposable container for the relatively incorruptible hereditary component, the "genotype," or genes. The body here is appearance, the genes the living essence. This conception is arguable, and offensive to many intellectuals, but it has a certain explanatory power. An explanation for the general blindness and madness of those in love, for men attracted to young women, to bodies, and women who find men with power and prestige alluring, is that they are sacrificing themselves for what goes beyond them, their sex cells that carry their genes into the next generation.

Together, men and women are the means by which sperm and eggs produce more sperm and eggs. The pessimistic German philosopher Arthur Schopenhauer wrote that the endless gossip, the constant attention paid to who is making love to whom, should be understood as a species demon contemplating the composition of the next generation. For modern social biologists there is no conscious species demon but rather the unconscious creativity of countless generations of replicating genes. The survival of animal species depends upon the sometimes shocking, often perverse behavior of the millions of animal bodies each of which houses hundreds to billions of demanding sex cells. We primates are late arrivers on the animal scene. As animals, as mammals, and as primates, we can be seen in the context of our evolutionary history and how the bodies of our primate relatives help reveal human sexual behavior in the recent evolutionary past.

Biologists like E. O. Wilson of Harvard and Robert Trivers of the University of California, Santa Cruz argue that genes determine major behavioral patterns in all animals, including people. From the point of view of social evolution, the genes of males and females require each other to reproduce, but such reproduction is essentially "selfish": insofar as the genes induce certain behaviors that produce offspring with those same genes in them, to that extent will the behaviors, no matter how vile or loathsome, be perpetuated. Philandering, for example, may be considered contemptible, but it clearly is an effective way for males to propagate their genes. Nor are females free of such genetic selfishness. On the contrary, the female who chooses a partner with genes that have a maximum chance of surviving and reproducing may propagate her genes too. The desire for such genetic benefits need not be conscious in people any more than it is in insects or rutting cervids. Pied flycatcher males that abandon their mates after providing them with nests and then pair with a second spouse produce on average 8.7 offspring, whereas faithful males produce on average only 5.4 fledglings. The biologists James and Carol Gould have suggested that the supposedly psychological phenomenon of male midlife crisis "may reflect an evolutionary ploy which directs men to abandon reproductively senile spouses, seek new partners, and rear additional offspring while they still have the chance."[6]

The unconscious evolutionary logic of males and females differs. Physiologically, if a man mated with a different woman every night he could sire thousands of children, whereas an equally promiscuous woman could bear at most some twenty children during her adult life. The dramatic variance in reproductive potential between males and females suggests that human males, unlike females, may have benefited significantly by copulating with as many lovers as possible. Thus, in males at least, the desire for "sex for sex's sake," the taste for sex without emotional attachment, very likely has been genetically reinforced. Cross-cultural surveys have revealed that women continually rank earning power before physical attractiveness as a trait important in a mate, while for men looks are far more a priority. That a single man can father hundreds of children by different women, while a woman can mother fewer than twenty children in her lifetime, is an explanation for the so-called Coolidge effect.

The Coolidge Effect

A glib anecdote illustrates the purported genetically based differences in the psychosexual orientations of men and women.

President Calvin Coolidge and his wife were taken on an agricultural tour. The guide brought Mrs. Coolidge to a chicken coop where she watched with extreme interest the amorous antics of a rooster atop a hen. How many times, she asked, could the rooster be expected to perform per day? The rooster, replied the guide, was capable in a day of performing intercourse dozens of times. "Please tell that to the president," said Mrs. Coolidge. By and by President Coolidge, touring separately, came to the chicken coops and was duly informed of the rooster's virility. "Is it with the same hen every time?" asked the president. "Oh, no, Mr. President—a different female each time," responded the guide. "Please tell *that* to Mrs. Coolidge," said Calvin triumphantly.

That men are by nature more willing to engage in sex than women is suggested by the greater promiscuity of male homosexuals compared with lesbians: it is as if, freed from having to compromise with the other gender, the natural tendencies of men and women are exaggerated with a clarity rarely seen in heterosexual relationships. A community health worker acquaintance from San Francisco told us of her first-hand experience with young men in the early 1970s. In confidential questionnaires on their sexuality, more than a few of her clients tallied over 365 different sexual partners in a single year. Men are also more likely than are women to fantasize about group sex or sex with strangers. Women are more likely to fantasize about someone they know, alone, in a serene setting. The difference is, it seems, an unconscious reflection of those strategies that are best suited to the genetic propagation of each sex. "Guys will," nightclub comedian Lenny Bruce once commented, "do it with anything, even mud." In many species, penislike appendages appeared as not-too-choosy males evolved ways to oust each other and inseminate the more discriminating females. An inequality in ancient means of sperm delivery—with some males preempting other males as they evolved means to get closer to the egg and shortcut external fertilization—led to the origin of the penis. Males who have retained their sexual "freedom" to engage in multiple female "conquests" sire the greatest number of children. Zoologist Donald Symons calculates that a male hunter/gatherer with one wife increases his number of offspring "an enormous 20 to 25 percent if he sires a single child by another woman during his lifetime."[7] Number of offspring is debatably the single most important ingredient of Darwinian success, the health of those offspring being another. Males that overcame female reticence and male rivals left the most offspring; they were the stars of our bawdy ancestry. "Small wonder," writes University of Arizona entomologist Robert L. Smith, "that selection has favored sex crazed human males."[8]

Avoiding the Sperm Contest

Jealousy, we said, because of its link to sperm production, sometimes acts as an intense aphrodisiac. But it can also be one of the most debilitating, hostility-engendering, and destructive of human emotions. In Shakespeare's play *The Winter's Tale* the jealous Leontes, King of Sicilia, becomes so deranged that he sabotages his entire life. Even though the king might be consoled in his jealous suspicions by the pregnancy of his wife, Hermione, every time she disappears offstage with the visiting Bohemian king, Polixenes, Leontes becomes ever more distraught, enraged, and unreasonable. Ultimately the Sicilian king persuades himself that the fetus his wife is bearing belongs not to him but to the Bohemian. Convinced that he has been cuckolded, Leontes now obsessively studies the face of his young son Mamillius for signs of likeness to the Bohemian visitor. Doubting his paternity, inconsolable, Leontes orders that Polixenes be assassinated, jails his wife, and refuses the boy Mamillius the right to visit his mother. The baby girl, born to Hermione in jail, is first sentenced to death, then abandoned to the elements upon Leontes' orders. Mamillius, deprived of his mother, dies, as does Queen Hermione herself. Leontes' jealousy has destroyed his family and himself. He is ruined by distrust, suspicion. No one can appease him, reassure him.

Why would an emotion so apparently debilitating and destructive as jealous rage ever have evolved? The social evolutionary reason is simple, perhaps too simple: the jealous lover is protecting his or her investment, guarding his or her genes. The problem is especially dire for men, who can make a lifelong emotional commitment to a woman, providing daily for her and her children, and yet be cuckolded in a matter of minutes. The vigilance of the jealous male seems to be a biological mechanism helping to ensure that any children produced will be his. This is why jealous males are often in the "rage mode," ready to kill rivals or use their superior physical strength to terrorize females into fidelity. For females the problem is less serious, since the cavorting male, while he may become involved with another woman, cannot be impregnated and therefore usurped as a genetic resource. A man, it seems, can never get quite enough assurance that only his and no one else's sperm has inseminated the egg of a woman, that he is the father. Today, genetic tests have been devised to assure paternity in the courts. But the problem of paternity assurance had far-reaching effects on humanity—and our ancestors—long before the inventions of writing and laws.

Tigers, bears, and some primates typically act like Leontes: they murder cubs they suspect were sired by another male, freeing up females to bear and care for their own offspring. Male animals who can ward off other males increase their chances of siring offspring, and therefore of safely delivering their own genes into the next generation.

The sort of sexual selection in which a reproductively successful male guards his females, frightens away or kills his competitors—or even elopes with his own mate—is not so much sperm competition as *sperm competition avoidance*. When Leontes, the sex-crazed Sicilian king, orders the execution of Polixenes, the king of Bohemia, he is avoiding sperm competition.

Despite their size and ability to instill fright, gorillas and orangutans have small penises, tiny testicles, and relatively scanty ejaculate volumes. The average gorilla penis measures barely over an inch when erect; the average orangutan's is only a fraction of an inch larger. Reproductively speaking, these larger animals do not need big penises and copious amounts of sperm. The silver-backed male dominates "his" fertile females in a gorilla harem, and other males rarely dare interfere with him. Although this top or "alpha" male permits others to enjoy sexual activity with subadult and pregnant females, his imposing physique and social authority ensure that fertile mature females within the group are off limits to his subordinates. The master thus has unfettered sexual access to the potential mother gorillas of his harem. Yet it should not be assumed that the dominance of primate harems is a male absolute; indeed, females sometimes play a crucial role in soliciting or electing new males to harems, of which the females often remain members longer than the "dominant" male. Since gorillas avoid sperm competition, large genitalia would confer on them little additional advantage.

Although orangutans too are "sperm-competition avoiders," they are slightly different. Loners who roam through the forests of Borneo, orangutan couples remain isolated after mating. In the jungle, usually alone or with a single mate, the orange-haired orangutans lead relatively subdued sex lives. Ergo their small genitalia.

The difference in body weight and other traits between males and females of a single species is referred to as "sexual dimorphism." Extensive sexual dimorphism reflects sperm-competition avoidance; relatively equal-sized male and female bodies suggest sperm competition. Studies of their bones show clearly that our ancient primate australopithecine ancestors were more sexually dimorphic and thus likely to have been sperm-competition avoiders. But the large dimensions of human male genitalia point to sexual permissiveness, to infidelities and orgies in our collective past: not all human ancestors were so sexually possessive as modern gorillas, or so isolated as forest orangutans. Considerable female promiscuity may have been our immediate primate heritage.

Promiscuous Chimps

Today human males employ

a variety of highly variable reproductive tactics, each mix depending on the opportunities to place sperm in competition and the need to defend against competing sperm. . . . The most common human male reproductive strategy involves attempts to monopolize sexual access to one or more women through pair-bonding . . . marriage will on average produce higher male reproductive return than any mix of other tactics that could be pursued at the expense of equivalent resources. . . . Prostitution, for example, is an institution that provides males the opportunity to make small cost highly speculative reproductive investments. If marriage is a blue chip stock, then intercourse with a prostitute is the reproductive equivalent of purchasing a lottery ticket,[9]

writes biologist Robert L. Smith. Prostitution, sexual orgies, and the gang rapes common during wartime are all rampant promoters of sperm competition, and, indeed, all these may have been more common in the past. But probably the greatest single source of sperm competition in the past was "facultative polyandry"—that is, female choice to mate with more than a single male.

Sperm competition may prevail in populations where all females are not continuously sexually active. Even though women are not chimps, these apes provide instructive examples. Female chimpanzees in heat undergo physiological changes: they become pink and swollen around the genitals and anus, and become very sexually active. British anthropologist Jane Goodall reported a chimp mother of four, named Flo, who became very excited during estrus, lifted up her pink buttocks, and mated with almost all the males in the troop.

Chimp females in heat are sexual athletes who will mate up to sixty times a day with twelve different males. Such behavior suggests that the nonhuman females may be seeking and achieving orgasms as they inaugurate intense levels of sperm competition. Amino acid sequencing—the study of detail in the chemistry of proteins that comprise our cells—reveals a closer kinship of humans to chimpanzees than to any other living species of animal.

Chimps share with people many genetic traits, including a male anatomy that may have evolved in the context of sperm competition. Although chimps produce more sperm per ejaculation than men, the sexual lifestyle of chimpanzees is probably more like our ancestors' than most of us would care to imagine. Indeed, according to anthropologist Michael Ghileri, human males share some essential forms of psychosexual behavior with chimps.[10] Ghileri, who studied chimpanzee society in the African rain forest, believes that because they are genetically related, chimp brothers and cousins allow each other to mate with their females. The communal bonding of related male chimpanzees may explain why they are so apt to share estrous females: according to the neo-Darwinian theory of "kin selection," the chimp male who impregnates a chimp female in heat wins also for his fellows, since the males are relatives that share many of each other's genes. Once thought to be tranquil jungle inhabitants, chimpanzees can be surprisingly aggressive, patrolling their territory, and killing strange male chimps. Ghileri claims that chimpanzee males expand their territory to obtain not only food but females. Moreover he holds that related *men* have ganged up to kill those genetically unlike them and to gain not only territory but genetically distinct women. Although to different degrees and on vastly different scales, a penchant for racism, sexism, and promiscuity seems to be common to both people and chimps.

The rape and pillage of wartime lend some support to Ghileri's sociobiological suggestion that men resemble chimps. Indeed, the effectiveness of killer bands of male relatives destroying "alien" men and marrying or raping "exotic" women helps explain, but not excuse, racism's dogged persistence throughout human history. If men especially are heirs to this terrible genetic legacy of inbred hatred toward those not like us, it would explain the prevalence in so many cultures of xenophobia, fear of strangers. Although dangerously cultivated during wartime, this supposedly genetically based ill will toward the other is visible also in films, where fictional strangers from monsters to mutants and evil extraterrestrials elicit terror roughly in proportion to how unhuman they seem. Thus, a humanoid, infantile alien such as "E.T." does not arouse the same level of fear or murderous feeling as Yeti, Sasquatch, or some invading unfamiliar life form.

If Ghileri is right, and we have a tendency to hate the stranger who is *too* strange, it may have been active earlier in evolution, when our *Homo sapiens* ancestors may have murdered off "brother" hominids closer to us in appearance than the ancestral stock of the great apes, who were presumably less threatening than our genetic brethren. But even if Ghileri's sociobiological horror story is correct, it does not mean that we are destined to sit by and watch. Even if we are predisposed to sexual violence and war against other races, our perception of who is "the other" can also undergo radical change. Already many ethnically diverse cities exist on this planet, whose citizens can easily be perceived as members of a single, human race. Global human survival now demands that we mollify any such genetically rooted cliquishness and culturally reinforced feelings of supremacy. And since, in fact, all humans depend for food on the genes of exceedingly nonhuman organisms such as the agricultural crops corn (*Zea mays*) and rice (*Oryza sativa*), it is not as if the minor genetic differences between humanity's tribes are in themselves insurmountable obstacles. We can, in other words, be participants in global cultural change, not merely "horrified spectators" of deep-rooted genetic predispositions.

Marriage and Monogamy

Different prehuman species suggest different levels of sperm competition. Judging from its teeth, *Australopithecus africanus* was certainly a vegetarian. Like gorillas, the vegetarian australopithecines showed a bigger difference in body size between sexes than men and women do today, suggesting that they were sperm-competition avoiders. Although no one, of course, knows for sure, Robert Smith speculates that physically imposing males bossed relatively sexually faithful females in australopithecine harems. These ancestors would have been very sexist, but the males, violently intolerant of promiscuity, would not have developed large genitals.

This sultanlike breeding behavior could well have undergone a radical change with the evolution of *Homo habilis*, "handy man": Smith postulates that subordinate *habilis* males, scavenging meat and offering pieces of it in exchange for sex, upset the earlier breeding system. The cooperative hunting groups that began with *Homo erectus*—our most recent evolutionary predecessor—ushered in relatively high levels of sperm competition. *Homo erectus* males were not much larger than *Homo erectus* females. *Homo erectus* was a communal species who not only gathered edible plants but hunted mammoths and used fire. Eating and sleeping together in groups— the sort of cooperative groups needed to hunt—may have made them far more social, more talkative, and better barterers than their sexually dimorphic australopithecine ancestors. And more promiscuous. It was with *Homo erectus*, Smith suggests, that people developed their relatively large male genitals. During the last two million years in Africa, male hominids lacking sufficient loads of sperm would have left few, if any, offspring. The pendulum then began to swing back: males, without losing their large testes and penises, were to become stricter, more repressed, and less promiscuous. Monogamous pair-bonding (or a strong tendency in that direction with males remaining more inclined toward polygamy) may have helped eliminate competition among males, thus strengthening the social group—crucial for life in the savannah. The promiscuous hunting system had sown the seeds of its own demise. Unequal distribution of meat could have led to "consortships"—one-on-one marriagelike relationships in which females accepted a steady supply of meat and in return remained relatively sexually faithful to their apemen beaux.

Human tendencies toward monogamy and romance may have begun as *Homo sapiens* males removed their fertile females from the promiscuous tribe. Such males assured their paternity by jealously guarding and devoting themselves to a single partner. At first such behavior, which to us seems traditional, was probably perceived as a threat to the social system: the daring chimpanzee male defiantly leaves his group, whisking his estrous partner off to the woods to be alone with her. Anthropologists report that today when chimp males reemerge from these "safaris," however, they may be beaten by other males—presumably for selfishly breaking the rules of the breeding game. Although a social ideal for people across the globe today, monogamy, ritualized by marriage, probably began as a perverse innovation—as elopement still seems to be in chimpanzee societies.

Human dating, monogamy, honeymooning, and the social codification of marriage may be classified as "take-over avoidance," part of a broad zoological spectrum of behaviors that have less to do with "love" than with maximizing reproduction. Geoff Parker has studied take-over avoidance in dung flies, creatures whose name immediately rebuts any incipient gushes of sentimentality. Nonetheless, dung flies do seem to "elope": males and females typically meet on warm crowded droppings but some pairs then fly off together downwind for a more intimate rendezvous in the cool grass. Since the upwind droppings are warmer, copulation is accomplished more quickly and with less metabolic effort on the fly-covered ordure. Eloping males, Parker reasons, make this considerable energetic sacrifice to avoid being taken over—knocked off their mates during mating.[11] In many species females benefit by the concentrated favors such as food offered her and her alone by an eloping male. Such females also may be spared the risk of bodily damage that often attends multiple matings.

Dung flies obviously are far more distantly related to us than chimpanzees. But the unconscious genetic reasoning, take-over avoidance as a survival strategy, seems to be strikingly similar in dung flies, consorting chimps, and honeymooning humans. As Parker rightly points out, the success of any particular mating behavior depends crucially on how others are behaving;[12] Parker has used the mathematical techniques of "game theory" to figure out how the optimal reproductive tactics change along with society and the rules of the social game. Looking at the social backdrop allows us to appreciate that there are no absolute or eternally optimal breeding strategies. Whereas chimps shuffling off into the woods, for example, are looked at askance and sometimes roughed up when they return, newlyweds in seclusion on a romantic interlude are abiding by the rules of the game. If society were as unchanging as the squares on a board game, there might be a single best means of reproducing for any pair. But society, composed of the individuals whose needs change and differ and whose mating strategies vary, is continually, if subtly, changing. As far as mating behavior goes, people were probably more like promiscuous chimps, but are now more like dung flies dropping out into the grass. Even though phylogenetically they differ greatly from us, the act of dung flies avoiding takeover is, like the elopement and erotic seclusion of newlyweds, an effective strategy in the reproductive game.

Flirtation can be distracting, promiscuity disorienting and confusing. Marriage, by contrast, is a stabilizer, publicly confirming the private passion. Did marrying humans outcompete their more promiscuous brothers?

Monogamous *Homo sapiens* tribes may have boasted better, more ruthless fighters than their libertine *Homo erectus* predecessors. As sperm competition declines, violent sexual vying between males becomes more important than high sperm counts or large penises as a way to secure male reproductive interests. The most prodigious sperm producer in the world dies childless if his genocidal associates prevent him from impregnating the women they control. In tribes of increasingly monogamous neanderthals and cromagnons—early members of our species *Homo sapiens*—sperm competition seems indeed to have declined. This decline may have been accompanied by an increase in aggressivity, war-making, and the spirit of revenge.

Patriarchy and phallocracy—the political rule of men— perhaps grew stronger when shamans danced; when big game hunters stalked, ate, and worshipped the animals they killed; when lovers coupled by lightning-lit fires; when people carved stones into deadly points, painted writinglike pictures in the damp, shadowy corners of caves—as men sacrificed to male or animal gods, stared in wonder at sun-bleached bones and the horn of the moon, and began to believe in the symbolic worlds they had invented. (Women, meanwhile, may have been doing the more crucial if less glorified work of gathering the majority of the food, creating pottery vessels, and bearing and rearing children.)

Part of the ritual violence of these deeply religious ancestors toward animals may have been their reinterpretation of adultery and infidelity as offenses, as insults to the father, as rips in the social fabric. Even today's antiabortion movement, which attempts to legislate and control reproductive behavior of women, may be part of this ancient swing away from promiscuity and toward phallocracy and male control, toward the prevention of sperm competition and the avoidance of cuckoldry by institutional means. When encroaching and receding glaciers forced our ancestors to reorganize and change their social behavior, human mating patterns may have undergone a shift such that sperm competition, the wanton promiscuity of the tropics, was no longer the norm; unsanctioned sexuality may have then become stigmatized as a punishable crime. Apemen became humans so recently, however, that the sperm-competition equipment bearing phallic witness to a more promiscuous past has had little opportunity to disappear. It hangs on, enigmatically, to different places, and an earlier time.

•

If early men—cromagnon and neanderthal "testosterone warriors"—monopolized power and wealth, early women may have submitted to them in exchange for protection and to provide for their children. We know that as late as feudal times it was a common custom for the lord of the manor to lay with his tenant's bride on what we would consider *her* wedding night. Although heralded as "gentlemanly virtues," adhering to values such as honor, chastity, and chivalry did not necessarily enhance a male's reproductive prowess. If morality as sexual fidelity works against a male's ability to sire as many children as possible, so fidelity does not ensure a woman will harbor her genes safely into succeeding generations. Nonetheless, monogamy might strengthen a *society's* potential for organized violence, including the destruction of other, more peaceful societies. *Homo erectus* males may not have been sufficiently vigilant in protecting women from impregnation by outsiders. Loving *Homo erectus* thus could have fallen victim to racism and sexism perpetrated by members of a more violent and jealous species, *Homo sapiens*. *Homo erectus*, evolving some two million years ago in warm latitudes, traveled north into Europe about 750 thousand years ago, taking pebble-chopper tools with them. These early humans made distinct hand axes; handedness, the human habit of preferring one hand, usually the right, and a corresponding specialization of the brain's hemispheres may have evolved in *Homo erectus*. As they made love and fires, their brains ballooned in size from 875 to 1050 cubic centimeters; as they engaged in group hunts and communal sex, the genitals of the males may have enlarged under the pressures of sperm competition. Studies of variations in the genes of the mitochondria of 100 living people suggest that the first *Homo sapiens* evolved 600 thousand years ago. The new humans, moving north, may not have been so promiscuous, but, probably under the influence of the first complex languages, they underwent rapid cultural change.

Charles Darwin was forced to grapple with the far-reaching (and theoretically unsettling) idea that not only individuals but groups and tribes evolve by natural selection:

It must not be forgotten that . . . a high standard of morality gives but a slight or no advantage to each individual man and his children over other men of the same tribe. . . . But a tribe whose members were always ready to aid one another, and to sacrifice themselves for the common good, would be victorious over most other tribes; and this would be natural selection. At all times throughout the world tribes have supplanted other tribes; and as morality is one important element in their success, the standard of morality will rise by natural selection.[13]

Animal bodies are groups of interconnected cells, many of which in tissue culture can still reproduce independently. Societies are groups of interdependent people. Incessant reproduction of cells—and cell death—is essential to the maintenance of healthy mind-bodies, just as the constant reproduction of people—and death—is essential to the maintenance of strong societies. Whereas an individual *Homo erectus* may have been more equipped than an early *Homo sapiens* man to impregnate a female, his attitude, his mood, and his lack of loyalty to a powerful fighting unit and politicized tribe may have spelled his downfall. Territoriality, male–male competitiveness, jealousy, possessiveness, ownership: these are not just the emotions of sperm-competition avoiders, they are founding rocks upon which much of modern patriarchal society is based. We can speculate that relative to dangerous *Homo sapiens*, our *Homo erectus* ancestors wallowed nonviolently in nonpossessive erotic love; they may have been more culturally stagnant precisely because they were less jealous, more sensual creatures.

Today we may be living in the aftermath of *Homo erectus*'s "failure." As the rules of the breeding game change, sex as a mode of human reproduction may also become a relic. In the heyday of *Homo erectus*, a million years ago, sex may have been a social glue in which everyone celebrated everyone else's lovemaking, and no one belonged to anyone else. But with later humans there came the matrimonial prisoners and wardens; there came laws, obligations, and possessive, punitive relationships. There is a tendency in evolution for modes of reproduction to become more and more restricted, as societies become more powerful and organized. Indeed, the human body itself is, in a sense, a society of highly organized cells, most of which have been stripped of their freedom to reproduce. In future societies only some people—chosen for the good of the "body politic"—may be permitted to reproduce. Birth control, homosexuality, environmental toxins, pornography, and artificial insemination have already distorted an ancient direct correlation between human sex and human reproduction. The thin, artificial membrane of the condom now separates the ancient connection between ejaculation and conception. From widespread incest taboos to parochial restrictions (including parietal restrictions of dormitories, celibacy vows taken by the Roman Catholic clergy, and spermicidal jellies), there has been a trend for fertile matings to decline. Restricting the reproduction of individuals can strengthen and spread the societies to which those individuals belong. Sexual repression and reproductive restrictions help explain why modern human societies have become the most deadly organisms on the planet.

We have changed, and are still changing, but not necessarily for the better. The hunting *Homo habilis* and fire-using *Homo erectus* from two million to 300 thousand years ago may seem morally reprehensible libertines. But were their forerunners, the australopithecines, who probably lived in groups in which a single male demanded and received sexual favors from a haremful of obedient females, any better? Do we embody this double lineage, on the one hand of violent sexism, on the other of pornographic excesses? It does indeed seem that we are caught between *Homo sapiens* possessiveness and *Homo erectus* priapism, between the rock of violence and the hard place of libertinism.

The possessive vigilance of modern humans had consequences. As we shall see, our adolescent female ancestors probably went into "heat": vaginally swollen, flaunting attractive scents and colors, they drew numerous male suitors. The loss of this estrus and the development of curvaceous, voluptuous, typically human breasts evolved in the context of primeval sexual deception. Females hid their real fertility from their sexually possessive mates, gaining favors from them. At the same time their curvy, nearly hairless bodies gave signs of being sexy and fertile almost all the time. Unable to time with accuracy when the young females were ready to be fertilized, the all-too-watchful males became unsuccessful at restricting the erotic activities of their mates. These changes induced watchful males to relax their vigilance, and allowed the females who had evolved voluptuous womanly forms—essentially forms confusingly mimicking both estrus and pregnancy or early motherhood—to enjoy food and protection from other males.

All humans alive on Earth today may well have come from the trick loins of females who concealed estrus. And from apemen who, though adapted to sperm competition, gave it up, at least partially, to elope and honeymoon with particular apewomen. The apewomen also competed—not for sperm, which was always, from their perspective, fresh and plentiful, but for commitment, support, and protection—for help with their crying infants—help that men were far more likely to promise than to give.

We have looked at men. Let us now trace the evolution of female apes into women, try to turn the flesh of the female body into text. The body of a woman holds within it clues to the reconstruction of her past history; the signs of evolution of her orgasm, pendulous breasts, and hidden estrus can be deciphered with a doubt and difficulty worth the effort.

2

ORGASM EQUALITY

> That whole societies can ignore climax as an aspect of female sexuality must be related to the very much lesser biological basis for such climax. . . . It is important also to realize that such an unrealized potentiality is not necessarily felt as frustration.
>
> —MARGARET MEAD

> I have read the female orgasm here as the privileged sign of female agency, where mind and body come together in female possession of the phallus.
>
> —DONNA HARAWAY

The stripper's cheek rests enticingly on her raised bare shoulder. Gently shaking to computer-composed music she begins a hyper-real holographic belly dance. Slinkily she removes a scarf to reveal her full-looking lips, which she licks, leaving them slightly parted and glistening. The electronic Mediterranean beat fills the auditorium as she performs a series of rhythmic pelvic gyrations that grow in intensity until they reach the level of orgasmic shudders. As she climaxes a man briefly appears beneath her, existing only long enough to ejaculate before disappearing again into her shuddering loins. In retrospect the audience realized that they saw her give ejaculatory virtual birth to a full-grown male. The body turned and below the rippling abdomen of the seven-veiled striptease artist was an obscure pubis, dark and hairy. The erect penis, the unmistakable signal of his sex, shrunk on the next rotation. It became the clitoris.

Now an apewoman vigilantly guards her toddler, her left arm supporting her newborn. Berry grabbing, seed cracking, branch bending, she looks up from shrubs to the maternal tasks at hand, out to the wandering toddler and down to the infant clutched at her left breast. The crackling underbrush bears loud tidings. As the brambles part and the face of a lone male appears behind them, she reads the lascivious expression. She knows all too well what he is seeking. She knows, too, what he knows: he sired neither. The babe-in-arms is not his child. The jump-stepping yearling-girl, now out of her mother's reach, is not his daughter either. Fearful for what he might do to her two light-weight offspring, the mother distracts him. She lustily stands spreadeagle. Slowly she turns and bends to expose her dark buttocks and the wet genitals below, bidding him welcome.

Male and Female Pleasure

The possibility of achieving orgasm with a partner acts as a powerful lure, influencing the behavior of both men and women. But whereas the genitals of both sexes are basically similar—forming a kind of "fun house" anatomical image of each other—the positioning of sexual intercourse can make it more difficult for women to achieve orgasm. Although there is a basic physiological equality between male and female orgasm, different cultures have attached different values to female orgasm. In this chapter we look at these cultural differences and biological similarities, and then explore the important role female orgasm may have played in human evolution.

At one of the outdoor habitats of the San Diego Zoo two monkeys mated in plain view. The male monkey thrusted several times, spun off the female's body, rolled over and began to sleep. The female, jittery and agitated, continued gyrating for some time. A small crowd watched in unseemly silent fascination, until one particularly mesmerized boy was suddenly whisked away by an older woman who had been captivated but now seemed overcome by modesty, disgust, or maternal protectiveness. Not only were the animals mating in public, but the female was abandoned to her dissatisfaction. The anecdote is not isolated. If inability of women to reach orgasm in a punctual manner frustrates male lovers, so "premature ejaculation"—the other side of the same problem, annoys not only women but female simians.

Vaginal Orgasm

Although female frustration such as that of the monkey in the preceding anecdote is probably very common in primates, a woman clitorally stimulated may experience many more orgasms than a man in a given period of time.

Although it is obviously impossible to compare directly male and female feelings of sexual pleasure, the question is intriguing enough to have excited theological debate. Teiresias, the only character in Greek mythology to have been both male and female, was called in to settle a dispute between Zeus and his wife, Hera, over which of the sexes achieves the greatest heights of sexual pleasure. Zeus held that women enjoy sex more; Hera begged to differ. Summoned to Mt. Olympus, Teiresias testified that women experienced nine to ten times the gratification of males. This answer so angered Hera she blinded Teiresias on the spot; Zeus, however, pleased, bestowed upon Teiresias a long life and the gift of prophecy as well, ensuring Teiresias's status as a Theban seer. This divine spat reminds us that the gods themselves are confused about the potential intensity of female sexual pleasure. Modern scientific study confirms that the capacity for sexual climax is a genetic potential of women. And if developed, orgasm apparently can envelop women in pleasures equal to or more intense than those of men.

But effective clitoral stimulation, though intensely pleasurable, does not necessarily occur during sexual intercourse. Female pleasure, far more than male pleasure, is a function of erotic learning and cultural expectations. Among human societies the most advanced orgasmically are purported to be the women of Mangaia, a southern Cook Island in central Polynesia. Mangaian females reach orgasm two or three times during intercourse. Upon entering puberty at thirteen or fourteen years of age, Mangaian boys go through a series of initiation rites into adulthood. Part of the initiation includes being instructed in methods of stimulating women to maximum sexual pleasure. Indeed, Mangaian women are expected to attain orgasm during intercourse each time; if not, the Mangaian man who fails to please her loses his status in the island's society. Two weeks after a manhood initiation ritual involving penile mutilation, an experienced older woman begins to practice boys in the arts of conferring female sexual pleasure. According to their ethnographer, D. S. Marshall, Mangaians probably know more about female anatomy than most European physicians. The Mangaians, with no semblance of a Puritan heritage, do not consider female sexual pleasure an indulgence. They consider it a necessity. High cultural expectations for female orgasm have led to high rates of female orgasm.

Until recently, the mainstream European and American attitudes toward female sexuality significantly differed from those of the Mangaians. Nineteenth century physicians mixed prudery with ignorance, recommending, on the one hand, that women not bathe, because of the potential hazard of accidental masturbation, while, on the other hand, occasionally prescribing regular douching as a covert means of stimulating spinsters whose ills were secretly diagnosed to stem from sexual frustration. There are reports of eighteenth century obstetricians operating sight unseen, under a blanket in a darkened room, out of alleged respect for the lady and her "private" parts. This embarrassed and embarrassing tradition results in

large part from biblical scruples condemning sex outside marriage or for reasons other than procreation. Under such a
prohibitive and proscriptive moral code, common human sexual practices such as fellatio, cunnilingus, and even foreplay
between married partners become condemned as sin or infused
with guilt. In the past century, European physicians had no
qualms about recommending that adolescents be tied to their
beds or administered chastity devices in order to prevent masturbation, which was thought to cause any number of disorders
ranging from physical weakness to mental retardation.

For all his brilliance, Sigmund Freud was a major perpe-
trator of such Western ignorance of female sexual anatomy.
Freud believed women were dysfunctional even if they *did*
enjoy orgasm. Freud held that while the erotic center of young
girls is the clitoris, as girls mature, excitation must be transferred to the "adjacent female sexual parts, just as—to use a
simile—pine shavings can be kindled in order to set a log of
harder wood on fire."[1] So convinced was Freud of the correspondence between mature sexuality and vaginal eroticism
that he defined *frigidity* primarily as the inability to make the
orgasmic transfer from clitoris to vagina. According to Freud,
unlike males undergoing puberty, pubescent girls experience
"a wave of repression"; the "clitoridal zone" must "abandon
its excitability." This repression and the necessity to switch
their primary erogenous zone from clitoris to vagina were "the
chief determinants of the greater proneness of women to neurosis and especially to hysteria."[2] With such a misguided view
of the vagina, whose inner walls are far less sensitive than the
clitoris, it becomes all-too-laughably clear how physicians
could prescribe twice-daily douching as a remedy for old
maids.

Freud's famous equation of healthy female sexuality with a
vaginal orientation, with a focus on the womb, upholds the
status quo; it keeps woman in her standard place as childbearer.
For whatever reason, Freud and his colleagues could not
accept that it was healthy for women to be clitorally pleasure-
oriented. Perhaps the idea of women motivated to please themselves solely for the sake of pleasure was threatening. If women

desired genital pleasure for its own sake and not necessarily for reproduction, polyandry would be legitimized; women chasing mates, including lesbians, to satisfy them, might become acceptable. Freud's speculations, codified as "fact" by the medical community, led to needless feelings of sexual inadequacy in three generations of women. Indeed, according to Freudian doctrine, even women who sustain multiple orgasms are "frigid" if their orgasms are centered on the clitoris.

Freud's theories were dismissed with clinical precision by sexologist Alfred Kinsey. "There is," Kinsey wrote, "no evidence that the vagina is ever the sole source of arousal, or even the primary source of erotic arousal in any female."[3] The clitoris plays the essential role in orgasm; contrary to Freud, mature, adult women routinely experience orgasms that are centered upon the small but very sensitive clitoris. Of course, today the situation has changed. Male sexual techniques for the achievement of female orgasm are discussed not only in private but on TV talk shows and in grocery counter magazines. Today's American women may feel inadequate if they do not reach orgasm, and their men feel the pressure "to perform." A large share of such pressure and expectation is idiosyncratic: a social phenomenon of our century and culture. Margaret Mead identifies entire well-patterned societies of subtropical and other peoples who, unlike the Mangaians—and unlike many people in the West today—put no clear value on female orgasm. They seem not to know about it. Not knowing about it, they do not miss it.

Some of the discrepancies, if not injustices, between human male versus female orgasm, are attributable to embryological constraints. Both men and women grow from unisex fertile eggs that become embryos. Each cell has forty-six chromosomes, forty-four of which are unrelated to whether the infant is biologically male or female at birth. The only visible sign that a fertile egg will develop into a boy is the lack of a tiny dark blob of chromatin (genetic material) within the membrane-bounded nucleus of the cells that develop from the egg. Females have forty-four regular chromosomes and two X chromosomes. Males have forty-four regular chromosomes, one X and one Y. Put another way, cells that will become baby boys lack the second X chromosome of females: substituting the missing second X blob is an inconspicuous Y chromosome in the cells of potential boys and men.

As the egg divides by cell division it forms the multicelled soccerball-appearing structure typical of all animals, called the blastula. The blastula then develops openings that expand and grow into tubes that become the mouth-to-anus digestive tract. When the human embryo first takes its form, the incipient penis and clitoris appear identical; they are the same unmodified unisex organ.

The penis–clitoris organ then modifies in utero. Derived from the same original embryonic structure, the penis and clitoris—in later fetal development—start to differentiate into their characteristic forms in response to chemicals circulating in the body—steroid and peptide hormones. Whether female or male hormones are released into the blood circulation depends on the chromosomes. The tiny second X chromosome in the nucleus of each of the cells in the body is the unmistakable sign of an incipient female. The replacement of the absent second X by a smaller Y chromosome marks each cell in embryos that become males. The genes, that is, the DNA comprising these chromosomes, produce proteins that switch on the production of a suite of either male-specific or female-type hormones. The presence in the blood of tiny amounts of these crucial signaling compounds, hormones such as the androgenic or male-producing testosterone, determines whether the penis–clitoris mound of tissue between the growing limbs of the human fetus enlarges vertically into a penis or horizontally retreats to become a clitoris.

Much later, at puberty, the release of hormones into the young adolescent's bloodstream causes further sexual differentiation. So-called secondary sexual changes—beards, breasts, pubic hair, and voice changes—are brought about by hormones. An interesting genetic ailment called "testicular feminization syndrome" sheds light on this process by its absence. Individuals afflicted with this condition are genetically male but do not respond to the first rush of testosterone delivered in the mother's womb. They thus appear to be and are often treated as little girls. (Their testes remain in the abdomen and they even have dead-end vaginas.) During puberty, however, they receive a second wave of testosterone, which does turn them into identifiable males: their testes drop, they grow a penis, and they develop a higher muscle-to-fat ratio. Biological sex involves genes, proteins, hormones, physiology, and development. The powerful masculinizing effects of testosterone can be seen in songbirds, the females of which, if treated early with hormones, are able to sing the complex songs normally associated with males. Likewise, female rhesus monkeys exhibit patterns of play behavior similar to males' when treated with testosterone. Hormones affect not only the body but the brain and behavior. Researchers using the magnetic resonance imaging scanner to look at soft tissue found that the corpus callosum, the "bridge" connecting the brain's two hemispheres, is larger in women, whereas the cortex of males is thicker in the right hemisphere. The hypothalamus, normally larger in female rats, can be seen to have undergone physiological changes after treatment with testosterone when viewed in thin slices under the microscope. To what extent we are "prisoners" of hormonal biology is unknown, although the datum that more than 90 percent of violent crimes committed cross-culturally are by men ominously implicates testosterone as the macho venom.

Fascinatingly, the extent to which gender is also a socially conditioned phenomenon is revealed by the fact that, in at least one culture, the Navajos, people with testicular feminization syndrome were not considered as being first girls and then boys, but rather as belonging to a completely different "third" sex. As Anne Bolin, an anthropologist at Elon College in North Carolina, points out, gender in many cultures is not simply "ascribed" (to genitalia) but "achieved" (socially). Bolin, who has compared the gender status of transvestites, transsexuals, and female body builders, makes the point that "culture often 'masquerades as nature.' "[4] Although we in the West believe the genitals are immutable insignia of sexual difference, different cultures give different meanings to the same biology. "Gender," as Bolin says, "is many splendored."

This cultural input to biological "truth" becomes ever more apparent with technological innovations. Transsexuals represent a new gender category in our culture of males on the way to femalehood. Yet transsexuals are neither. Some begin as males, who then receive oral and sometimes intramuscular injections of the female hormones estrogen and progesterone. They develop breasts and fatty tissue on their hips. Hormonally reassigned and surgically converted, they undergo a kind of second puberty, for which no clear rite of passage yet exists. Transsexuals dismiss drag queens, female impersonators, and effeminate homosexuals as ersatz, artificial, imitative women, whereas they, with their hormones and breasts, come closer to the real thing—even if that real thing remains more in the line of a "third gender" than a biologically born woman. Although some state governments merely scratch out the old names of transsexuals and add new ones to existing personal documents, others such as Louisiana issue transsexuals brand new birth certificates.

There are famous rumors of sexually prodigious eunuchs and castrati, operatic singers castrated at puberty to preserve their high-pitched voices. Giovanni Francesco Grossi, for example, was supposedly murdered in Italy in 1697 on the road between Ferrara and Bologna for carrying on an affair with the countess Elena Forni. Some doubt these stories, however, since castration before puberty can cause primary hypogonadism, a condition resulting from the lack of increased production of androgen (testosterone) hormones in the interstitial Leydig cells in the testes at puberty.[5] Because of this condition, emasculated singers may have been blessed with voices sweeter than a woman's, but burdened by an infantile penis, an underdeveloped prostate, "eunuchoid" (disproportionately long) arms and legs, beardlessness, pubic hair distributed in the female opposed to the male pattern, and fat deposits on the hips, buttocks, and breast areas. Indeed, in 1792 the renowned ladies' man Jacques Casanova wrote of a castrated homosexual favorite of Cardinal Borghese who supped every evening with his eminence and played the prima donna at the theater. "This *castrato* had a fine voice, but his chief attraction was his beauty. . . . On the stage in woman's dress . . . he was ravishing, a nymph, and, incredible though it may seem, his breast was as beautiful as any woman's; it was the monster's chief charm. However well one knew the fellow's natural sex, as soon as one looked at his breast, one felt all aglow and quite madly amourous of him. To feel nothing, one would have to be as cold and impassive as a German."[6] So, too, whatever their gender, eunuchs may have surprised sultans, though not concubines, with their lovemaking powers: seminal fluid, but not sperm, can be produced in the absence of testicles.

More recent candidates for the possibility of a new culturally recognizable gender include women body builders. The cells of female body builders, whose low-fat diet and androgen injections may lower their voices and lead to their expulsion from women's rooms, contain two X chromosomes; genetically female they display a splendidly different gender. We applaud Bolin's cultural relativism, which is a good reminder of the limitations of biological science.

Both traditionally recognized sexes have structures biologically indispensable to the other that are leftovers of embryological development in their own. Organs such as nipples, crucial to breast-feeding women and useless in men, fall into this "embryological leftovers" category.

Penis and clitoris begin as one and the same tiny undifferentiated organ, but in the Y-chromosome-bearing male, circulating steroid hormones, especially testosterone, induce its enlargement to become the penis. In young intrauterine humans, the two labia majorae—the outer vaginal lips—are at first indistinguishable from the scrotal sac. While in females the two lips remain apart, in the male a generalized structure enlarges, folds over, and, fusing along the midline, becomes the scrotum. The clitoris is a kind of unenlarged penis. It has a quality of "extraness" owing to its inessential relationship to conception, just as, in the male, the residual midline of the male scrotum is a vestige. Both make sense from the viewpoint

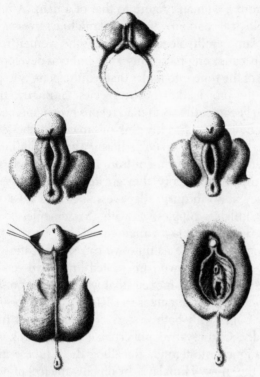

Human males are indistinguishable from females at first, in utero: both have mounds of tissue where their genitals will later appear (top). The tip elongates, becoming the penis with its foreskin, and the sides fuse along the midline and swell to become the testicles in the male (left), whereas in the female the tip differentiates to form the clitoris and the sides become the vaginal labia (right). *Drawing by Christie Lyons.*

of evolution, which uses hormones to modify the unisexual embryo; both evince a kind of graceful economy, as if they were designed by a genetic inventor whose artistry was strapped by limited resources.

Aristotle compared animal embryos to the rough sketches of a fine artist before they are filled in with lifelike details. The midline of the scrotum may be conceptualized as such a line, the leftover trace of another drawing, the mark of a pen many of whose other lines have been erased in the rapid transition from a woman's figure to that of a man. A relic of the embryological economy, the scrotal midline serves no purpose. In this same embryological economy the woman retains her clitoris because originally unisexual embryos develop some 50 percent of the time into males that require penises to play their part in the propagation of the species. Similarly, the infant boy who becomes the adult man retains two pigmented patches on his chest; he retains his pink or brown flat-chested nipples because his mate must suckle her newborn. The infant's imperative to suck nourishment from its mother renders a man's useless nipples obligatory; they are an undeveloped evolutionary legacy of no intrinsic adaptive value. And yet stimulation of their milkless nipples, as with the semenless clitoris for women, is pleasurable for many men.[7]

Extending Aristotle's simile we can say that the male and female embryos are, with no wasted lines, two versions of a single elegant sketch. Indeed, that which renders one version male and the other female is so slight it would appear that the master, frugal with both erasers and ink, knows his pen is almost dry. Conservative and crucial, the black ink is like the sex hormone testosterone. Recalling the Chinese artist who painted the snowy Himalayas by dipping the feet of two chickens in paint, and then dragging one (the mountains) and letting the other walk (the snow) across a scroll, tiny drops of well-placed ink or circulating hormone render economically subtle differences between male and female.

Sexologists and others deceive themselves with the preconceived notion that nature must be just. The anthropomorphic Judeo-Christian belief that God designed men and women in His image is antithetical to the Darwinian notion that evolutionary processes are entirely devoid of foresight. There is no universe designer who measured, cut and fit, and perfectly matched the sensitive male organ of sperm delivery to its patient egg-retaining receptacle. Nature often appears closer to autism than artistry. Nonetheless, some researchers claim clitoris and penis make a perfect match; they imply that these two little blood-filled muscular organs were "meant" for each other.

Probably unbridled optimism rather than faith in divine design led to the acceptance of the idealistically egalitarian sociosexual claims prevalent in the 1960s. Whereas society changes rapidly, anatomy is conservative—a disparity that leads rapidly to disenchantment. The possibility of mutual sexual orgasm does not mean that it can be easily achieved, or that the clitoris is ideally placed for lovemaking. Satirist Alix Kates Shulman parodies the wishful thinking of the sociosexual egalitarians: "Masters and Johnson observe that the clitoris is automatically stimulated in intercourse since the hood covering the clitoris is pulled over the clitoris with each thrust of the vagina—much I suppose as a penis is automatically stimulated by a man's underwear whenever he takes a step."[8] Evolution is not headed toward perfection. We do not inhabit the best of all possible sexual worlds. Evolution is spastic, an "epic tale told by a stutterer" (Arthur Koestler's simile). It is no master creator but a bumbling basement tinkerer (François Jacob's view). Natural selection of the fertile male's penis produced—by opportunistic, unpredictable evolution—the corollary unenlarged structure, the clitoris, in his daughters. The clitoris is thus not, to put it crassly, God's gift to women.

Nature has no grand plan. "Natural selection" indeed is merely the failure of all possible offspring that are born or hatched to persist and reproduce in the game of life. Life, all life, is potentially prodigious—the selection or persistence of the few through time resembles less the will of an omnipotent creator than the scrambling of a klugy computer programmer. ("Klugy" is computer talk for a program that is not well designed or even well understood but has, rather, been meddled and fiddled with until it works.) Even if it did evolve in the shadow of the penis, once it appears as a sensitive organ or instrument, the quivering clitoris is still capable of being tinkered with and finding a function. Like an unused circuit board or extra wall switch on a cluttered toolbench, the clitoris does not necessarily have an evolutionary purpose. Indeed, one hardcore evolutionary view is that the clitoris is not needed ever for anything. Our view is that although it appeared at first just as a legacy, as an "embryological leftover," the opportunities for evolutionary invention were so rich that such a useful little mechanism was eventually put to use within the complex framework of human evolution. The clitoris is not, as is the penis, absolutely required for reproduction. Moreover, as the long shadow of the future begins to loom on the horizon, we begin to realize, in these days of artificial insemination, that even the penis may one day be reduced to a minor role in the human reproduction process. If biotechnologists could reliably clone human beings, the penis would be put in a position similar to that of the clitoris now: fundamentally an organ of pleasure, and only secondarily one of reproduction.

The Clitoris in Culture

While inessential to reproduction, and probably not directly selected for over the course of evolution, the clitoris is crucial to a woman's sexual pleasure. In this, the pleasures of the clitoris are more like music, art, or love, more cultural, more in the realm of human play, less involved in evolutionary work than those of the penis. The fine arts, the pens and pencils and paints of the old masters are themselves of no use to survival; but we may enjoy them immensely. Survival and aesthetic values do not always agree. And that is the rub; what has evolved need never have been selected. Although the result of evolutionary history, not everything in the organism, even the supreme pleasure of the female orgasm, is an adaptation for survival.

Animal lovers, investigators of behavior, ethologists, and graduate students have amassed a plethora of observations of vertebrate sexuality. Such zoological evidence, taken together, helps develop a coherent picture of the past history of orgasm.

Female orgasm seems relatively rare in the animal world. Female animals do not lack clitorises, they just seem in general not to have discovered them, perhaps because they are not stimulated in the rear-entry interior position almost universal for nonhuman mammals. "Compelling evidence of nonhuman female primate orgasm has been obtained only among captive animals. . . . In each case in which there was compelling evidence for female orgasm, the orgasmic female obtained direct and prolonged stimulation of her clitoris or clitoral area, either by experimental design or by rubbing against another animal."[9] A female rhesus monkey reaches back and clutches her mate at the moment of ejaculation; chacma baboon females vocalize when the male stops thrusting; stumptail monkeys have been observed gazing back at their lovers with a "positive emotional expression." But passion is not necessarily orgasm. Female orgasm among primates in the wild appears to be the exception rather than the rule. On the other hand, reactions such as those just stated suggest that females may well be capable of orgasm, the males just inept at regularly providing it.

To understand changing views of orgasm in female primates, it is important to realize that evolutionary science does not occur in a vacuum but is immersed in Western cultural history. Drawing on medical writings, it has been argued that before the late eighteenth century, female orgasm was considered to be necessary for conception, and that "[T]he 'problem' of the clitoral *versus* vaginal orgasm would have been incomprehensible to a Renaissance doctor."[10] Although in the 1960s primatologists considered female orgasm among primates to be rare in the wild, in the 1970s female primate orgasm in the wild was reevaluated and considered to be more likely, in part due to reports by Suzanne Chevalier-Skolinkoff of extensive heterosexual and homosexual mounting among stumptail macaques in captive colonies at Stanford. In her book *Primate Visions*, Donna Haraway suggests that this reevaluation of the likelihood of female orgasms in the wild was not the neutral result of disinterested scientific observation, but integrally connected to the Women's Liberation Movement, in the early years of which, "orgasms on one's own terms signified property in the self as no other bodily sign could."[11]

Female orgasm became a symbol of female worth—a kind of womanly gold standard—independent of the values of males. "Orgasm becomes the sign of the mind, the point of consciousness, of self-presence, that holds it all together well enough to enable the subject to make moves in the game, instead of being the (marked) board on which the game is played."[12] "Like their human cousins," Haraway writes, "primate females seem to have been born into the post eighteenth-century liberal world of primatology without orgasms and as natural altruistic mothers."[13] Female monkeys and apes got their orgasms back in primatology just when women did in society; monkey and ape females were perceived as agents or actors on the evolutionary stage just at the time when women were becoming more empowered in society. Here, as elsewhere, when we hold up the mirror of nature, we see a disguised reflection of culture.

Darwin's Oddities

Charles Darwin boarded the famous vessel *Beagle* in 1832 with the notion that he would confirm some of God's excellent designs by scrutinizing the lush tropics of South America. Far from finding evidence that each species was created separately by a divine creator, Darwin corroborated the views of a major if uncredited mentor: his poet grandfather Erasmus, who held that all earthly life forms were the multifarious offspring of a single tenacious ancestor.

On and off the ship for five years from northeast Brazil to Tierra del Fuego and the Galapagos Islands off the coast of Ecuador, the younger Darwin became fascinated with the strange imperfections of nature. Penguins with flippery wings slid into the water on their bellies, unable to fly. Praying mantises methodically tore smaller edible insects apart limb from limb. Tortoises waddled into the soups of hungry sailors. Finches with their array of beaks, each suited for a different sort of food, in particular caught Darwin's eye. The striking diversity of these closely related island birds suggested they evolved from a common finch ancestor—just as Darwin knew that distinctive breeds of dogs had evolved from a common wolflike stock. Darwin followed up on his hunch that the oddities and irregularities, the imperfections and quirks reveal the circuitous routes of history. Evolution did not walk in straight confident steps toward a predetermined goal, rather the ramblings and meanderings, the unique turns, stops and occasional about-faces were enigmatically displayed in the undesigned bodies of living things.

The weirdness, cruelty, and makeshift way in which organisms seemed "made" for their environments caused Darwin to doubt that any benevolent Creator, should He (or She) exist, had anything like a blueprint, grand plan, or design. Darwin is supposed to have dealt a mortal blow to contemporary pride when, by compiling a wealth of data and publishing *The Origin of Species*, he cast humanity as an extra on the stage of existence, ousting us from our lead role as fallen angels costarring under the headliner God. In fact, although historians often pay lip service to Darwin's "Copernican revolution"—his decentering of humanity—few have realized the extent to which we are mere bit players in the global ecological theater, cast among crowds in the cameo, or at most, supporting role of upright, large, and chattering apes. We may have a special role to play in earthly ecology, but our role is nowhere near as special or unique as many would like to think. If man is made in the image of God, either there is something terribly wrong with the imaging process, or God Himself bears all the marks of an imperfect and irreducibly historical evolution.

Opposite or "Neighbor" Sexes?

In the best of all possible sexual worlds, a woman might experience orgasm during intercourse with the same ease and on the same timetable as her man. But the real world of coupling bodies is not the work of a vengeful Father or omnipotent prankster; it is a work of fits and starts, of half-measures and biochemical evolution. It is to this world of imperfections, the half-hewn evolutionary mixture of Heaven and Hell that the enigma of the clitoris belongs.

One writer who rejects the placement of the clitoris outside the vagina where it is not directly stimulated during coitus is the infamous Marquis de Sade, one of whose heroines possesses a huge clitoris with which she penetrates, thrusts, and enjoys orgasm in the manner of a man. But such droll scenarios remain fictional. Women in today's life may experience themselves as less than man, if not as an "appearance enveloping a hole,"[14] then as a victim of phallocracy—the sexist rule of men and their ultimate if unacknowledged ruler—the phallus. Men, after all, still rule the biological literature, too. Perhaps this persistent cultural injustice or gap manifests itself by the desire of some women to posit real evolutionary importance— some survival-oriented raison d'être—for the clitoris and its none-too-certain pleasures.

Historian Thomas Laqueur argues that prior to the eighteenth century—in classical times and during the Renaissance—a "one-sex" model of human sexuality prevailed in which men and women were considered "neighbors" rather than "opposites." Early anatomical illustrations depict the vagina (the "neck of the womb") as an internal or inverted penis, and male and female private parts were indistinguishable insofar as they were referred to in several languages by common names (*orcheis*, *didymoi* denoted both ovaries and testicles; "purse" in Renaissance English meant both scrotum and uterus). In this model of a single, shared type of human body, both men and women were imagined to need to ejaculate in order to conceive offspring; male semen was considered to be a particularly concentrated foam or froth of the blood that appeared in women as menses. But as Laqueur shows, even in this earlier one-sex model, women are thought of as lesser beings, as inferior, incompletely realized renditions of the male prototype.[15] Women, since they shared a universal body microcosmically corresponding to the heavens, were not separate, but they were still unequal. Though largely replaced, the arcane one-sex model lingers on, informing, for example, contemporary embryology. But phallocracy, according to Laqueur, has not been scathed by the radical change in the way we view our own bodies in relation to the "opposite" sex. And for Laqueur the underlying cultural-historical models of sexuality guide rather than follow research in disciplines ranging from endocrinology to evolutionary biology.

Intermittent Rewards

While evolutionists like Stephen Jay Gould and Donald Symons believe that female orgasm "is not an adaptation at all," the zoologist John Alcock argues that the clitoris "does something." Female orgasm, Alcock opines, "is *not* an imperfect, half-hearted imitation of male orgasm, but a strong physiological response that is different in pattern and timing from male orgasm."[16] Whereas Gould suggests that naive evolutionists mistakenly assume that intercourse naturally triggers clitoral orgasm, when in fact there is no such pelvic harmony, Alcock accuses Gould of saying that "orgasm must serve the same function in women as men."[17] But there is an alternative, says Alcock. The "failure" of frequent predictable orgasm need not preclude an adaptive function for it. Ventral intercourse, in which partners face each other, and in which the male pubic bone stimulates the clitoris more effectively than the rear-entry positions of most other mammals, increases the woman's chances of achieving sexual climax. Although she may not climax every time, or at all, when she does, her orgasm may be qualitatively different—indeed more extensive, longer-lasting, and more pleasurable—than a man's.

The "jackpot" theory of human female orgasm was put forward by psychologist Glen Wilson.[18] Rather surprisingly, experiments in behavioral psychology have shown that animals rewarded with a treat (such as food, sugar water, etc.) are more likely to trip a lever if the treat released by tripping the lever is provided *only sometimes*. Female orgasm is a phenomenon Wilson implicitly compares to the thrill of gambling, and his theory is named after the human analogue of such behavioral psychology experiments, slot machines that occasionally gush forth silvery streams.

Women who experienced orgasm prior to their men were tempted to disengage before ejaculation, decreasing their odds of becoming inseminated and pregnant. Such women, quickly and easily satisfied, bored before their lovers had climaxed, would have left comparatively few offspring; presumably few descendants of such women are here today. The continued presence of premature ejaculation in the human species is accounted for by the ability of fast ejaculators to impregnate females before they are themselves satisfied. Other, less easily pleased ancestral women would nonetheless have "hit the jackpot" of orgasm occasionally. These women received intermittent rewards of genital pleasure and thus were incited to repeat lovemaking, to go back to the "reproductive gaming tables" again and again.

In outline, Wilson's "jackpot" theory is that female physiology drives women to lovemaking as addictively as a gambler to the dog track. Female orgasm acts as a motivator of bedroom behavior not despite but because it occurs intermittently, according to Wilson. Intermittent feedback, rewards delivered unpredictably, are notoriously good at motivating animals to repeat behavior, if not to develop addictions. The weakness with Wilson's theory is that animals without orgasm also mate, and bear offspring. Why should an "orgasm addict" be any more successful at transmitting her genes? What is the advantage, if any, of fickle pleasure, orgasms experienced powerfully but inconsistently?

Far from linking sex partners in a faithful relationship, the dissociation between orgasm and intercourse encourages a woman to enjoy sex with several men, thereby preventing any one of them from injuring her babies: this is, at least, the argument of primate biologist Sarah Hrdy. Men interested in a woman's sexual favors will be reluctant to attack her babies. Infant murder is an act commonly committed not only by lion and tiger males but by male anthropoids; presumably it increases the killer male's reproductive success by more quickly siring his own offspring. Many pregnant mammals not only show no interest in sex but cannot conceive if they are nursing their infants; infant murder renews the cycle of menstruation and fertility. Hrdy suggests that ancestral pregnant females, by consenting to sexual intercourse, may have protected their vulnerable children against infanticide; female sexual pleasure, sex for sex's sake, would have been adaptive to primeval females. In an animal world where female genes can be transmitted only by coupling with males so brutal they may kill babies in order to receive sexual attention from females that would otherwise be distracted by mothering, it helps to be able to desire clitoral orgasm even while nursing and caring for infants. Hrdy paints a picture in which prehistoric female orgasms, by making females interested in sex year round, saved females from potentially homicidal males and the terrible genetic waste of destroying an infant in which so much had already been invested.

But for Stephen Jay Gould, Hrdy's quest to find *any* reason for the clitoris is misplaced, since the clitoris is simply the by-product of an originally unisexual embryo. According to Gould, "No one is more committed than Hrdy to the adaptationist assumption that orgasm must have evolved for Darwinian utility in promoting reproductive success."[19] Hrdy writes of the clitoris:

Are we to assume, then that it is irrelevant? . . . It would be safer to suspect that, like most organs . . . it serves a purpose, or once did. . . . The lack of obvious purpose has left the way open for both orgasm, and female sexuality in general, to be dismissed as "nonadaptive."[20]

The problem remains that if we assume orgasm's importance to reproduction, why do many female mammals (who have clitorises) reproduce perfectly well without any noticeable orgasm? The problem is less to explain the "jackpot" form of occasionally overwhelming sensations of pleasure, than to explain why female orgasm exists at all, if it is not necessary for reproduction. Female climax, according to Symons and Gould, is no more an adaptation than male nipples. It is a coevolved legacy, the result of genetic momentum, of a neutral feature riding "piggyback" on a useful one. Though it provides pleasure, the clitoris, in this view, is as superfluous as the appendix: it makes no significant contribution to human reproductive survival.

Nonetheless, the genetic momentum view of orgasm in women as evolutionarily neutral has been challenged: female orgasm may indeed increase survival. According to Hrdy, while female orgasm is not necessary for reproduction, it is adaptive for survival of offspring; therefore a male in a polyandrous society would do well to choose a highly orgasmic female, since his offspring would have a better chance of surviving other male threats.

Another idea of the importance of orgasm from the viewpoint of female genetic survival comes from biologist John Alcock. Orgasm in Alcock's view is not needed to induce women to mate more often. After all, several copulations suffice for a woman to bear a handful of children, and thirty seconds' worth of pelvic thrusting can lead to a lifetime of parental responsibility. Rather the importance of female orgasm to reproductive success comes, Alcock suggests, from its ability to enhance paternal care. Human infants are so helpless at birth that women who can assure themselves of a devoted or at least providing husband have a distinct evolutionary advantage. If a father who cares for his child also cares whether or not his partner experiences orgasm, a woman can use the one to gauge the other. If good, orgasm-producing lovers, in other words, make good fathers, then in the event of conception, orgasmic women seeking out such lovers would have benefited. Orgasm-attaining women would have discriminated among potential fathers. By choosing good lovers, they ensured that their babies would have been better cared for.

The emotional component of female orgasm is crucial. Women secure in their relations with their partner may be more likely to regularly experience orgasm. One study, for example, suggests that contemporary call-girls or high-class prostitutes who work from their own homes achieve orgasm as frequently as other women do, whereas prostitutes who walk the street climax with greater difficulty. Probably the wealthier, generally more secure professionals who enjoy more reliable and attentive clients are less exposed to the exigencies and dangers of urban street crime. If female orgasm indeed helps women choose the fathers of their children after they have mated, then such disparity between privileged prostitutes and impoverished streetwalkers might be expected. Professionally obligated to mate with unreliable strangers, streetwalkers in shying away from orgasm unconsciously avoid its attendant increase in risks of pregnancy, emotional attachment, and childrearing under conditions of destitution.

Perhaps the simplest explanation of female orgasm's survival value comes from Richard L. Duncan. An amateur biologist, Duncan is a curious businessman who became enlightened after speaking with an ex-U.S. Air Force man "who had the exceptional personal experience of socializing with many women in many different countries over a period of twelve years."

Duncan remarked upon the common experience of women standing up after intercourse and having the semen drip out of their vaginas and down their legs. Such loss of semen, Duncan surmises, was a problem in the prehuman move, about four million years ago among the australopithecines, to an upright posture: sperm, unaccustomed to fighting gravity, must have been laid to waste by the untold millions in the simple gesture of females rising to their feet after sex. Keeping the woman recumbent, either by the male continuing to thrust after ejaculation, or by the female resting after intercourse and perhaps especially after her orgasm, would enhance the chances of fertilization.

Whereas females may have exerted control over their reproductive fate by encouraging sexual intercourse in a frontward position, men would have preferred the rear-entry position traditional in quadrupeds including our four-legged ancestors. Rear-entry intercourse may be a favorite position of men (if it is) because intercourse in this position spurts sperm that contacts the cervix directly and tends to bypass the vagina. Semen shot deeply and directly to the womb is less likely to be dislodged by standing up, and it is more likely to come into contact with an egg. (Direct contact with the cervix as well as the suction effect of female orgasm that we shall examine shortly suggest that the best way for a woman to become pregnant is to have the man assume a rear-entry position while the woman achieves orgasm.) Because it tends to deprive them of the little reproductive control they still retain, women would not be as fond of this position as men. The contrast comes from the surmise that males who preferred rear entry, the position that has the greatest probability of fertilization, would have sired more offspring like themselves; females, however, would have favored a variety of positions depending on their desire to become pregnant. The tendency toward upright posture—and loss of semen—was counteracted by the tendency of the satisfied female to reach orgasm and then rest afterward on her back long enough to give the sperm a fighting chance. One should also consider the predilection of humans to make love at night and then to sleep—horizontally.

The Suction Effect

Perhaps the best evidence of an evolutionary function for female orgasm comes from experiments that reveal that a woman's orgasm increases her intrauterine pressure.

This increase in pressure leads her body to unconsciously suck in more sperm, resulting in an augmentation of the chances for successful fertilization.[21] No reliable means of contraception existed before condoms, the birth control pill, the diaphragm, and the intrauterine device (IUD). Promiscuous women or rape victims likely to be impregnated by men undesirable as fathers would have benefited by developing means of decreasing their likelihood, after mating, of conception. Female orgasm, or rather its absence, may have been an early, if unreliable, aid in birth control.

Monitoring copulating humans in the laboratory, Masters and Johnson found that face-to-face intercourse is the best means of stimulation unto orgasm in coitus.[22] During the peak of female orgasm, the outer part of the vagina rhythmically contracts from three to fifteen times, the inner end of the vagina expands, and the uterus, too, reversibly contracts for several seconds. The hormone oxytocin, released from the woman's pituitary gland in response to clitoral stimulation, may mediate these genital responses. The pleasurable contractions transport semen from the vagina to the uterus, raising the probabilities of fertilization. Positive intrauterine pressure is generated during coitus and becomes negative after female orgasm. This pressure decline creates suction, propelling sperm into contact with eggs. These data suggest that women may actively draw sperm toward their egg when they climax— giving a reproductive advantage to the sperm of males who bring them to orgasm, or with whom they choose to achieve orgasm. The contractions of orgasm may even, like a vaginal "door" slamming shut, serve to block out subsequent males as they welcome in the sperm of her favorite.

As part of an unconscious wisdom of the female body, female climax enhances fertility; if established, this "device" would help expand female reproductive options. Some women undoubtedly conceived children via orgasm-inducing lovers outside their accepted conjugal relationships. Adulterous women often enough became pregnant by other men, and clitoral or vaginal orgasm may have fixed the odds, allowing the sperm of a good lover or desired mate to take precedence over the sperm of a husband, despite the latter's primary sexual access. Presumably some of these extramarital partners had "better" genes. Men, throughout the evolution of the species, by their larger stature and greater physical strength, tended to overpower females. Raped women, or those compromised by exchange of sexual favors for food or social mobility, may have decreased their chances of becoming pregnant by avoiding or feigning orgasm with reproductively undesirable men.

In a climate of male brutality, orgasm would have given women a bit of control over their biological destiny, mitigating the barbaric rule of men as they sought greater control of their reproduction, consciously or not. Since the greater physical strength and differing genetic interests of males existed no doubt prior to humans, optional orgasm and other female sexual behaviors could be reproductively important for millions of years, from australopithecine girls to the twenty-first century women who ultimately derive from their furry australopithecine loins.

Female orgasm's fertilization-enhancing function may even be detectable in the sexually satisfied Pacific people of the island of Mangaia.[23] In an ordeal of initiation into manhood undergone by all young Mangaian men, the urethra of the penis is slit in a fine cut toward the scrotum. The natives call the mutilation *mika*—the "terrible rite." The subincision would tend to make the semen dribble out, and this would seemingly decrease the occurrence of fertilization among the Mangaia. The young men, meticulously instructed in the arts of love, are taught to delay their ejaculation until the moment of female orgasm. According to Robert Smith, Mangaian culture takes such pains to instruct its mutilated men in erotic technique precisely because they are mutilated and therefore less fertile: the spermatic impairment and the orgasms would tend to balance each other out and reestablish a normal level of fertility. If female orgasm sucks in sperm, then the effects of the ejaculatory debilitation could be countered by the women. This may explain the importance mentioned earlier of achieving orgasm with each copulation, and the frequency of sexual intercourse, which is reportedly indulged in by Mangaian married couples at least once daily.

Wilson's "jackpot" analogy, Hrdy's notion of orgasmic interest protecting females from killer males, Alcock's idea that the good lover is the good father, Smith's suggestion of enhanced fertility, Duncan's hypothesis of horizontality: each of these explanations of the benefit of female orgasm seems to us about as good—and difficult to prove—as the others. Indeed, even the views of adaptationists and the nonadaptationists need not be mutually exclusive. Gould may be correct when he compares the existence of the clitoris to the existence of male nipples, and traces the raison d'être of both to requirements for reproduction in the opposite gender, namely penises and lactating breasts. But given the human penchant for quick learning, the clitoris also may have evolved to play a role in reproduction—becoming crucial when human ancestors began walking upright, and when thoughtful females sought more control over the fathers of their children. Nonetheless, if orgasm in women evolved any role in evolution, it is still relatively minor compared with that of the imperative of the fertilizing effect of ejaculation of sperm through the male penis.

Metaphysics of Sex

We conclude that in its early evolution the clitoris had no evolutionary significance; it came into existence because of the advantage its counterpart, the penis, gave sperm-competing males. In sexually reproducing species, males and females can differ significantly in size, coloring, and various bodily adornments. But because both sexes develop from the same embryo, because they are variations of the same original embryonic "design," the two sexes can never be completely different. Like the tinkerer's extra bulb and battery leading to new inventions, the retention of the clitoris led to clitoral orgasm, which allowed greater female choice in the selection of mates. Infants—always at risk—may also have been better protected by mothers whose men were willing to indulge them in clitoral orgasm. Natural selection retains male penises and ejaculations; males are born of females whose embryology they share. From an evolutionary perspective, it is the presence of the penis in the male that gives the female the opportunity to quiver in delight as she releases spermless streams.

We have seen how the penis and clitoris begin as the same embryonic organ. But human sexual response differs considerably from male to female: the anatomical similarities between male and female genitalia are not in accord with the different patterns of male versus female orgasm. These differences can be brought into accord if we take a close look at human development. Sexually immature, prepubescent boys enjoy a range of sexual response similar to that of adult women. Kinsey and his coworkers reported, "The most remarkable aspect of the preadolescent population is its capacity to achieve repeated orgasm in limited periods of time. This capacity definitely exceeds in the ability of teen-age boys who, in turn, are much more capable than older males."[24] The responses of young boys, including multiple climax without losing an erection, "is," according to biologist Donald Symons, "perhaps similar to orgasmic women." Neither prepubescent orgasmic boys nor women ejaculate sperm, and thus the "ability of females to experience multiple orgasms may be an incidental effect of their inability to ejaculate."[25] Both anatomically and physiologically the clitoris seems to be a diminutive version of the penis.

To what extent is this evolutionary argument based on unexamined—and perhaps objectionable—metaphysical presuppositions? Female babies, for Aristotle, were imperfections, incomplete males whose *telos* or goal had been frustrated. If the sperm were hot enough, Aristotle mused, the male principle could withstand the coolness of the mother's body, and the seed would develop "fully" into a boy. For Aristotle, the *catamenia*, or menstrual fluids, were impure; unlike male semen, they lacked "the principle of soul." The view that the clitoris is an embryologically incomplete version of the penis strikingly recalls the Aristotelian view that the woman is an incomplete manifestation of what becomes complete only in and as man.

Aristotle's thoughts grew out of the soil of Greek culture. Ancient Greece was a society in which only men were fully empowered; foreigners were considered barbarians and women debased along with slaves. In such a society—a conscious model for the West—it was far easier to think of a man mothering a woman than it was to conceive of a woman "fathering" anything. In a strange reversal of the actual relative contributions to the production of offspring, fathering in Western metaphysics is considered primary, primordial. Zeus is the king of the gods, and the Judeo-Christian God is also male, a father who makes man in his own image. In this grand delusion, to father is to create, whereas to mother is simply to nurture, to incubate, to protect for a time.

Some of the Greeks believed that manly nobility, or *arrete*, was contained in the semen and could be transferred privately or publicly (for instance by anal intercourse, at the Temple of Apollo) to young men. Long before Freud, in the second century A.D., Artemidorus wrote a book called *The Interpretation of Dreams*. In its analysis of dreams, it reflects sexual attitudes 2000 years old. If a man has sex with a prostitute in a dream, according to Artemidorus, this may portend death. The reason is found often in the sexual tenets of philosophers: sperm, considered valuable, is here wasted, used in a way that will bring no return in the form of offspring or heirs. Eastern warnings against the waste of sperm, as well as advice to warriors not to have sex before battle, may have a biochemical basis in the use of prostaglandins both in brain function and sperm production. In Greek and other languages, terms used for sex may ambiguously also refer to economics. *Soma* means body as well as riches and possessions, for example, implying a possible confusion between possessing a partner's body and acquiring wealth. *Ousia* in ancient Greek means both substance (or presence) and semen, so that there is a ready equivalence between loss of (in English: "spending") sperm and incurring some sort of cost. So, too, *blabe* refers both to economic setbacks and the assumption of a passive or victimized role in sexual activity. These terms relate to a cross-cultural and perhaps even, as in the baboons, cross-species equivalence between sex and roles of dominance and subservience within social hierarchies. They also suggest a history for sociobiology's male-oriented love affair with terms of sexual and reproductive expenditure, such as "evolutionary costs" and "paternal investment." Pedagogy, educational instruction, and pedophilia, the erotic love of young boys, were once interdependent. Although the ancient Greek culture was more tolerant of male homosexuality than our own, belief in the superiority of males may be relatively unchanged since before Aristotle. So inscribed into our culture is the presupposition of male supremacy that it is retained even in the roots of Western science. In this metaphysical matrix, woman is base matter, man valuable information or form.

The Hindus thought of the agricultural furrow as a vulva, the seeds as male semen. One ancient Indo-European source states, "This woman is come as living soil. Sow seed in her, men." Another declares "Woman is the field, and men the dispenser of seed."[26] Here pedagogy as writing, as the imparting of information, is linked to the male shaman or priest, who possesses the disseminating pen, the regal staff, the magical scepter able to represent, confer, or create the Truth with a capital T. There is a deeply held conceit that the male's phallic objects are somehow the true fatherly source beyond all female things. This cultural prejudice holds widely, from the preponderance of male authorities and experts to the phallic monolith left on the moon as a message to humanity from an alien life form in the film *2001*. And yet this ultimately metaphysical determination that information flows along male conduits, that knowledge is of the father, seems fundamentally flawed—more like the ironically impotent bauble of the fool than the sovereign scepter of the king! If in the context of informational flow of evolution, we reflect on the lineage of cells from the first until today's, we are equally justified in considering the informational flow of life as maternal or feminine. But it is also a mistake to consider the asexually produced offspring of fissioning bacteria "daughter cells." Perhaps we are most justified in considering life's informational flow genderless, since the earliest bacteria, passing information around the world and changing gender as they received it, were already beyond all limits of the male/female false dichotomy.

Aristotle's metaphysics of sex were embraced by Christianity through the influence of Church-father Thomas Aquinas. In the seventeenth century Antoni van Leeuwenhoek, a draper from Delft, Holland, constructed his own microscopes from lamplight and glass beads. Van Leeuwenhoek peered down in fascination at his own recently ejaculated sperm cells. Directed by an ancient and sexist metaphysics, van Leeuwenhoek thought he had detected parts of microscopic homunculi— tiny male beings—swimming in the whitish fluid. Unsure of himself, the Dutchman wrote to the Royal Society of London that it would be better to find "an animal whose male seed will be so large that we will recognize within it the figure of the creature from which it came."[27] The very word "spermatozoan" comes from "seed animal"—as if the seed of the human animal were already contained in the sperm and the woman merely a disposable vessel, a fertile medium, a sperm receptacle, a formless substance, a chaos to be given shape and meaning by this highly ordered and ordering cosmic "seed"—male sperm.

Today we know that the woman's egg cell contributes more than half the information of the new human-to-be; it gives not only twenty-three nuclear chromosomes to complement the twenty-three of the sperm but also contributes all the cytoplasmic DNA—the mitochondria whose genes come entirely from the mother. This startling fact rings like a death knell over the ancient pretension of the reproductive eminence of the father. In modern biology, the male has lost his pride of place. Like his counterpart in society, he is being given over to the feminine whirlwind.

Machine Genitalia

In a "sex scene" in the science-fiction comedy film *Sleeper*, Woody Allen takes his place within a circle of intimates and is passed a hissing electrified orb, called an "orgasmatron." He handles the electrified orb, whines histrionically, and then passes it on, as if it were a peace pipe among a group of Native American chieftains. In the less intentionally comical film *Barbarella*, postmodern women indulge in sex for fun; they pop pills to become pregnant. Whatever one may think of their quality, both films project an almost complete divorce of reproduction and eroticism; both depict a "disentangling" of propagation from pleasure. The dissociation of sexual pleasure from reproduction is probably a prerequisite for the evolutionarily common move from crowds to organisms at a different level of organization such as when green algal cells came together to make colonial forms. The original ability of the individual constituent cell to reproduce on its own is compromised and sacrificed to the loftier reproduction of the multicellular organism as a whole.

Human beings are perhaps in the midst of a similar epochal development, in which, if current population trends continue, individual reproduction will become successively sacrificed to societal reproduction; individuals, most no longer reproducing, may specialize to perform separate functions necessary for the greater life of the society. Aldous Huxley projected this scenario in *Brave New World*, in which a totalitarian government used lower-caste humans brain-damaged from birth by alcohol to perform menial tasks and reserved the right to reproduce only for the elite; indeed, a similar situation—of a society most of whose members do not have the ability to reproduce, a society that we thus see caught on its way, frozen in the state of becoming an organism at another level—exists in various species of bees, ants, and other social insects. True, people are not insects. But we are ultimately collections of what once were microbes. Not only organisms but groups of organisms reproduce.

Female orgasm may play a role—albeit more subtle than that of the male—in the reproduction of human beings. But if reproduction of individual human beings is itself curtailed owing to the need of reproducing human collectives, then orgasm could go its own way. The flame of orgasm may be "stolen"—like the fire that Prometheus took from the gods and gave to man—and applied beyond its ancient evolutionary setting of lovemaking between fertile humans. More and more a hedonistic indulgence, orgasmic pleasure may split from human reproduction altogether and be "exapted," as the biologists say, for other functions.

The body's track to orgasm is so sure, in both men and women, that the roles to which orgasmic pleasure might one day be applied transgress even the limits of pulp science fiction. Sexual pleasure might be exploited by nonhuman interests to reinforce desired human behaviors. Science fiction writers have imagined "smart" spacecraft that rendezvous once a generation to breed their human maintenance workers. Sexual pleasure may become so far removed from its human reproductive function that the experience of orgasm will someday be offered as a feedback, reward, or credit for the production of a nanotechnic chip or the performance of behavior considered valuable to future ecosystems. Already the extent to which multinational advertising in the global electronic media associates mass-market consumer products with erotic satisfaction could be considered an augur of the shape of things to come. Only erotic appeal and not yet genital satisfaction has been manipulated for ends other than human reproduction, but if the pleasure centers of the brain involved in orgasm ever come under the powers of global legislation and policymaking, beware! The psychoanalysts Freud and Otto Rank have discussed how the greatest cultural achievements are partly the result of sublimated sexual desire; how personal neurosis, so debilitating to the individual, can be rechanneled into society and transformed into the art that gives that society identity and power. Integrated into postindustrial technologies, the capacity for sexual pleasure may well outlive the coupling of human lovers.

We tend not to be aware of how, already, we are sexually involved in the production of machines. We have yet, argued Samuel Butler in the nineteenth century, to see the fruitful union of two steam engines. A steam engine does not directly give birth to a steam engine, nor an iron nail another nail. Nonetheless, like a flower that needs the pollinating bee to reproduce, human products reproduce through the agency of human beings. We are already on highly intimate terms with machines. Indeed, our current society could not continue without machine proliferation, without the rampant production and consumption of products, without our national dependencies on manufacture, our collective thirst for devices of convenience from food processors to sleek automobiles, our lust for laser printers and sensuous blowdryers, our coveting of clothes, shoes, and other items of sexual fashion and social status. It is a mistake to blindly assume that because human products and machines come later and depend upon the organic replicative chemistry of human beings, they do not reproduce: we evolved far more recently than the cell organelles upon which we depend, such as the maternally inherited mitochondria. No one, however, would protest that humans do not "really" reproduce. Biological reality may indeed be as strange as science fiction: sexual energy and other human pleasures *already* serve a function in forms of living organization that include the "reproduction" of machines. The pleasures of shopping and consumption drive the mass production of synthetic polymers, multicolored packages, and plastic and metallic items of many kinds. Teenage Mutant Ninja Turtle toys give a futuristic thrill to children. There is a widespread adoration of military artifacts and space vehicles, and a still greater intoxication with computers and related electronic systems ranging from laser disk stereos and cyberspace headsets to magnetic resonance imaging machines and the latest lifesaving medical technologies. Our pleasure in using such toys, systems, products, and machines is the best indication that they will continue to be marketed and (re)produced far into the future.

•

The trip has begun. Four million years ago the humanlike australopithecine Lucy shuffled through the tall grass in East Africa. Named after the Beatles' song "Lucy in the Sky with Diamonds" (which shares its initials with the powerful hallucinogen LSD), Lucy, dressed up, would look something like a short, slight, hunched-over woman. But she wasn't dressed, she was hairy from head to toe, all four or so feet of her. Paleontologists know she was a woman from the shape of her pelvis. And they deduce that she strode upright, belly and breasts exposed, despite her small skull and chimpanzeelike face. Because she walked upright, or slightly stooped, semen would have dripped out of her when she stood up. Lucy, and ancestral mothers like her whose skeletons were not preserved so completely, are our ancestors; they may be the source of many of the genes in the nuclei of your cells at this very moment. They were fairly flat-chested (probably, breasts do not preserve in the fossil record) and small-brained, but because they walked upright, they faced each other and males; face-to-face intercourse, coitus with stomachs touching, lips kissing, and eyes gazing became more likely, as did female orgasms and communicative, talking relationships. Since females are probably more likely to become pregnant if they climax, the orgasms of Lucy and other *Australopithecus afarensis* females may have helped organize the gene pool of what was to be the human race.

On the one hand, modern-day people are partly the result of the sexual choices and pleasures of ancient females. On the other, there is no such thing as "modern-day people": we are our ancestry, who and what we *were*. We spoke of cultural prejudices masquerading as biology. One arbitrary prejudice we take for granted as a fact of life is our notion of death, and birth. We say that somebody is born when he or she comes out of the mother and the umbilical cord is cut. The Chinese, however, consider a person to be already nine months old by the time he or she emerges from the mother. If we follow this logic through it becomes clear that our notion that the embryo and the eighty-year-old are one person while the parent and the child are distinct individuals is somewhat arbitrary. Memories fade but the DNA of our parents and great-great-grandparents all the way back to Lucy and beyond lives on in us. In a sense, the skeleton of Lucy is not that of a dead person; it is part of our living ancient self, a strange transgenerational husk, like the discarded pupal or caterpillar forms left behind in the transformation from insect egg to butterfly.

Webster's Dictionary traces orgasm from the Greek *orgasmos*, itself from *orgon*, "to grow ripe," be lustful; akin to Sanskrit *urira*, meaning sap, strength. And the sap, the strength of our ancestors, has not run out. Their ancient actions reverberate to this very day. The show goes on.

3

BODY ELECTRICK

Be not ashamed, woman—your privilege
encloses the rest, and is the exit of the rest;
You are the gates of the body, and you are
the gates of the soul.

—WALT WHITMAN

A poet looks at the world as a man looks at a woman.

—WALLACE STEVENS

It is always *as if* I had committed incest.

—JACQUES DERRIDA

With a whirling turn the evolutionary stripper reveals that the human body itself is a piece of clothing. Another twirl and the body reappears: her swollen rouge and violet vulva, the object of desire of her mate. The mate, a large broad-foreheaded agile male with a youthful face swings into view, scanning her horizons above the purple vulva. He hungrily seeks the pendulous breasts of his half-remembered childhood.

Body Games

Reconstructing the changes of females from Lucy-like ape to modern women is a difficult enterprise. But according to the best guesses of evolutionary biologists, during the multimillion-year evolutionary metamorphosis from hairy, flat-chested ape to modern buxom woman a major principle was at work. Males were kept guessing about when females were ovulating. Once their females' fertility waned, males would tend to leave them; this is why it was so important for females to keep males in the dark. An abandoned female had a much more difficult time tending her infant than one who shared child care with a devoted male. Given the sexual interests of males, females whose bodies lost a distinct period of heat and provided fewer clues of when they were ovulating could expect more sustained attention from males. They were better protected, more amply provided for, and, most important, their children—and therefore their genes—fared better. The argument claims a genetic advantage for females whose bodies were ambiguous, cryptic, enigmatic. Ancestral lovers apparently played not only mind games but body games. They unconsciously advertised and disguised themselves, showing signs of sexual readiness, chastity, and pregnancy. With phallic noses and everted, vaginalike lips they captivated each others' interest, lured each other into caresses of furless skin, and romantic, involved relationships. Women enchanted men with their rotundity and curves, becoming sexually attractive virtually all the time—and therefore eluding the attempts of selfish males to mate with women only when they were ovulating.

Another part of the story, speculative but crucial, concerns the highly impressionable state of human infants, the males of whom seem to have developed a sexual liking for "maternal" females—females that reminded them of their nursing mothers. Sexual imprinting, in which the young memorize features of their parents, and then seek out those features in mates when they mature, is prevalent in animals. Male mallard chicks, for example, use their mothers as a sexual model; if experimenters remove their mothers and expose them to stuffed male mallards during the critical period of sexual imprinting, the male chicks will grow up to prefer male partners. Female mallards, by contrast, do not imprint upon their fathers, because although he helps build the nest and incubate the eggs, the father departs before the eggs hatch. Scientists believe that the cues that attract female mallards—the iridescent green head and violet wing color of the male—are innate, prewired into the avian nervous system, not imprinted cues. A similar system of sexual recognition, although more varied because of our complex brains, may be at the root of human erotic attractions. If early, impressionable human infants imprinted on their nursing mothers, males would have grown up with a confusing lust for women who were not ovulating, but lactating. Genetically disadvantageous to males, this confusion would have been a genetic advantage to females who, sexually attractive almost all season round, stood a better chance of keeping fathers to help with children.

Nietzsche may have had an inkling of this sociobiological idea of an ambiguous female when he wrote:

> . . . supposing Truth is a woman—what then? Are there not grounds for the suspicion that all philosophers, insofar as they were dogmatists, have been very inexpert about women? That the gruesome seriousness, the clumsy obtrusiveness with which they have usually approached truth so far have been awkward and very improper methods for winning a woman's heart? What is certain is that she has not allowed herself to be won.

Of course, this conception of woman as the incarnation of the elusive, common to some philosophers and sociobiologists, is a very male perspective.[1] But evidence of the unconscious cunning of female bodies is not merely a male fantasy.

Gender-based physiological deception can reach extensive proportions in certain species of monkeys. In langurs, for example, males typically control a harem of females, and, whenever a new male takes control of the harem, he usually kills all the young present. Since pregnant and nursing mothers do not ovulate, this infanticide works to the murderer's genetic advantage by bringing mothers back into estrus—the colorful genital swellings indicative of ovulation—so that the new male can impregnate them. The marauder will also kill babies born soon after his murderous intrusion—babies that cannot possibly be his.

But against such relentless male brutality, the female employs a remarkable device: if a female is recently pregnant, and a new male kills her mate, she will sometimes go into "pseudo-estrus"—*falsely* advertising her fertility when, in fact, she is already pregnant. With swollen red skin and other lures working their physiological magic she mates with the male intruder, presumably to fool him into thinking that when the offspring are born, he is the father. The anatomical charade of pseudo-estrus is not exclusive to female langurs. Indeed, pseudo-estrus or at least behavior of sexual receptivity at a time the female could not have been ovulating has been documented for a variety of monkeys and apes. These include rhesus macaques, patas, Japanese macaques, chimps, vervets, and gorillas in captivity.[2] In what is known as the Bruce Effect, rat females spontaneously abort if they even smell a new male who has been introduced in their absence into the cage. The rodent abortions seem to be a genetically expedient means of saving the time and energy that would be wasted if the offspring were brought to term only to be killed by a strange male. The pseudo-estrus of monkey females is a vast improvement on this desperate rodent bailout, since it preserves the females' genetic investment even though it involves a form of bodily lying. The whole bewitching socioevolutionary notion of females misleading males by bodily trickery is reminiscent of Nietzsche's half-paranoid feeling that life, in its modesty, naiveté, dissimulation, in its endless play of appearances, of veils and masks, resembles a woman.

Other physiological deceptions demonstrate how gender foolery need not be restricted to a single species. There is a kind of burrowing, near-sighted beetle from South Africa, the males of which are duped not by females but by flowers. When the males emerge in the spring, they promptly attempt to mate with the delicate petals of a local species of orchid. The orchid's petals resemble females of the beetle species, and the flowers produce an aroma very similar chemically to the sexual perfume naturally emitted by female beetles. The result of such excessive lovemaking is that the orchids are cross-pollinated, while the myopic, love-sick male beetles still succeed in reproducing later in the spring when their same-species mates emerge from the thawing ground.

The imperative of meeting members of the opposite sex has led to any number of evolutionary imbroglios. One species of fireflies exhibits the characteristic lighting patterns of females of another species: when the second species come to seek out mates, the first species unceremoniously eats them. Another example of interspecies seduction involves humans. Truffles, subterranean fungi that grow among the roots of oak and hazelnut trees, depend on mammals for their dispersal. Alleged aphrodisiacs, truffles were once distributed through the woodlands of Gaul through the activities of wild boars; primeval French chefs employed boars to locate the gourmet treats. But today truffles, especially the Perigord truffle, which is the prize of *haute cuisine*, are ferreted out by trained bitches and sows. Only female pigs and dogs sniff out these fungi. Indeed, since truffles contain alpha-androsterol, a male steroid hormonelike compound, these females may be under the false impression that they are on the trail of a member of their own species. And since alpha-androsterol is found in the underarm sweat of men and urine of women, it may induce a subliminal sexual effect or subtle added attraction to the other gender. In fact, in one study men rated pictures of the same clothed women higher when the photographs had been first secretly daubed with alpha-androsterol.

Ancestrally linked to estrus, sexual excitation, and the mating act, smells in general still influence our personal behavior far more than we are aware. Our tastes are mainly determined by olfaction. The human sense of smell has not disappeared even though its importance in primate communication has decreased relative to its central role of the wet, sniffing snout of nonprimate mammals. Indeed, nearly all of us powerfully respond to armpit and genital scents. Although we are still limited in comparison to our canine pets, the range of our scent-inspired actions probably expanded during prehistorical and even historical times. The mode of our "nasal appraisal" and details of our scent detection behavior moved away from smell's early status as a means of sensing the readiness or not for sexual intercourse, broadening into the realms of artifice and culture as humans evolved. The smell of the infant head is still an innate cue inducing a mother's immediate and fierce protectiveness; but now perfume, smoke, or ethanol fumes may bind initiates together with the glue of familiar smells. Subtle odoriferous cues change our relations, enhancing intimacy or hastening repulsion toward freshly scrubbed acquaintances. Women exposed to each other's body smells may menstruate at the same time each month, although the physiological mechanism and evolutionary meaning of this anatomical conspiracy remain unknown.

That a person can look attractive and smell bad, or vice versa, suggests the important status of smell as an independent sense once linked powerfully to mate selection. But as with vision, the sense of smell may also be misled: witness the vast sexually oriented merchandising of such olfactory distractions as antiperspirants, colognes, and scented shampoos.[3]

Tail Feathers and Pubic Faces

In some species of birds, females mate preferentially with long-tailed males. The shimmering iridescence and extension of the peacock's feathers exemplify traits that may have been selected not because they offer any survival advantage to the peacock, but because they please, sexually excite, or otherwise charm the peahen.[4] Sexual selection is a form of natural selection: one gender selects for traits in the other. Ironically, but typical of the unplanned vagaries of evolution, traits found alluring and chosen by one gender may be to the detriment of the survival of the other. Brightly colored fish, for example, attract not only mates but predators.

Darwin believed that the difference in skin color and skull shape among the races, the difference in nose shape and the distribution of body hair among various peoples, were all the result of sexual selection. For Darwin the lack of body hair in humans compared with the "Quadrumana"—monkeys and apes—was on balance detrimental to survival but arose when semihuman males chose females with increasingly less hair on their bellies and fronts. This is an example of male choice. The relatively hairless women tended then to transfer their traits for nakedness to their male offspring. Differences in skin color, the result of aesthetic preference, not primeval prejudice, arose after the skin had begun to become denuded of hair and thus visible—in a selective process analogous to the one that produces the necks of some tropical birds, necks that are featherless and highly decorated with colors and stripes. Beards, by contrast, were selected by the half-human female progenitors of our species because they appealed to them as ornaments, in the same way that the often pure white, yellow, or reddish patterns of facial hair in monkeys were selected for by female monkeys. Members of one gender may become so intoxicated with a bodily fashion that they select for the same pattern of shape or color scheme in different parts of the body. The fire-engine red nose and yellowish beard of the male mandrill mimic the color scheme of his bright red penis and yellow pubic hair, not to mention his pale blue scrotum. Similarly, in humans, some have suggested that the phallic appearance of some men's noses, and the scrotal look of some men's clefted chins are not accidental but the result of female selection. So, too, the coiled or wiry texture of facial hair, present in men far more than women, hints at primeval female selection of pubic-looking male faces.

Darwin concluded that sexual selection had been "by far" the most important agent in forming the differences among races, each of which had its own standard of beauty despite a universal taste for a certain degree of variety. Nonetheless, Darwin waffled when it came to deciding which gender had exerted the greater influence upon the human form. Evolutionary biologists generally agree with Darwin, that in most species of animals the female does most of the choosing of mates. Humans differ from most other mammals in that females generally have the most striking appearance. In the lion, the stag, the mallard, and many other species, by contrast, the male dazzles with his "dressing up." The countenance of the lioness and doe is relatively drab. The assumption has been that fertile females—in shorter supply—tend to choose the most gorgeous-looking mates. Female sexual whims thus can gradually incarnate themselves, materialize in the form of male bodies. In an ironic reversal, the real-life fashion show seems to consist of female designers, while males strut across the evolutionary platform, showing their stuff. More so than in males, the direction of the future physical and behavioral evolution of many species is under female control.

Experiments have borne out the importance of sexy bodily features. The Swedish biologist Malte Anderson attempted to find out whether the presence of long feathers was really a trait that captivated romance-seeking female fowl. To test this supposition, Anderson behaved like an avian beautician: he clipped off the tail feathers of male African widowbirds *(Euplectes progne)* and glued the cuttings onto other males to make their tail feathers longer. The black-and-red males normally grow long tails, up to four times their body length, during mating season. No less than the effects of high-heeled pumps or whale-bone-stayed corsets on young women, the long tails hinder movement of widowbird males. Yet the same barbered males with artificially extended tails mated more often than they had before the cutting and gluing. This contrasted with the birds with clipped tails and the males who were left untreated, both groups of which scored the same when their mating success was tallied.[5]

Human beings respond to potential mates by such superficial signs—parts that stand for wholes. The tail feathers of the peacock or widowbird are only a part of the bird-brained fowl, but to the peahen the bright feathers reliably signal the reproductive worth of the male as a whole. This is the idea of "advertising": that sexually selected characters such as prominent tail feathers are associated with the health or vigor or what Darwin called the "fitness" of the animal that sports them. But since parts are more easily altered than wholes, the evolution of charming reproductive attributes may serve—like the careful application of makeup, cosmetic surgery, or tailored suits with shoulder pads—to mislead the other gender as to the desirability of the mate in question. Clothes enhance the opportunity for such misdirection to an extreme degree—as in the case of transvestites who sexually attract heterosexual men.

Such human experience is not unique; dishonesty in sexual advertising and "cheating" is rampant throughout nature. Some bluegill sunfish behave like Tony Curtis and Jack Lemmon when they dressed as women to hide from thugs in the Marilyn Monroe film *Some Like It Hot*. They are "transvestites." Appearing to be harmless females, they swim about unattacked by strongly territorial males. Physiologically disguised and safe, they then disseminate their own sperm within the den of less cunning males. In short, physiological deception is prevalent throughout the animal kingdom. Any animal that can perceive can be deceived. And the deception need not be performed sneakily, at the level of the plotting mind, but can work unconsciously, at the level of the evolving body.

Among those female traits that probably fell from primeval fashion in the transition to humans were the colorful swellings of "heat" or estrus, still present in baboons, mandrills, drills, macaques, and other monkeys. The two enlarged nipple-tipped mounds called breasts also distinguish women from female chimps, female gorillas, and female orangutans. So do the buttocks, which, in contrast to the monthly ovulation-associated swelling of the rear ends of monkeys and apes, remain permanently "swollen." The hymen, a thin crescent-shaped covering over the vagina of most virgins is unknown in monkeys, apes, or any other animal. Like face paint and poetry, the hymen, breasts, and loss of estrus are trademarks of our species. And all seem to have evolved within a climate of acute perceptions—and therefore acute deceptions—between ancestral male and female humans.

Males good at detecting, quickly fertilizing, and impregnating females were rewarded by persisting throughout evolutionary history. Any clue to female reproductive readiness was valuable to the male who learned to recognize it. Although ovulation is patently obvious in many mammals, including some thought to greatly resemble our primate ancestors, even today neither women nor men easily identify an ovulating woman. If human males detected the release of eggs, allocating the resources they usurped by superior strength and political power to preserve their reproductive interests, they would seek to mate only with ovulating women. Avoiding speculating on nonovulators they would tend to spurn the mothers of their children most of the time. But it appears, as we shall see, that women's bodies have prevented men from knowing when they were ovulating. Most mammals are motivated by the prospect of mating only during mensual or seasonal estrus, periods when mating results in pregnancy. Many female mammals permit copulation only during ovulation. Women differ markedly from most other mammals by experiencing a peak in sexual pleasure and desire just before the onset of menstruation—a time when they are unlikely to become pregnant.

Bloated Breasts

Among the mammals, only human females develop mammaries that become full-looking at puberty and remain swollen whether or not they are producing milk. Estrogen induces growth of adipose and stromal tissue, filling and fattening the breasts permanently after puberty; such permanent enlargement is in stark contrast with the mammaries of apes, which only look full when they are full of milk.

Some highly imaginative theories have been advanced to explain the peculiarly human phenomenon of woman's breasts. For Desmond Morris, author of *The Naked Ape*, female breasts imitated "a pair of fleshy, hemispherical buttocks" in order to "successfully shift the interest of the male round to the front."[6] The paired pink or brown globes supposedly made "the frontal region more stimulating,"[7] encouraging face-to-face intercourse, which, according to Morris, helped "bond" couples into parental units, augment the chances for female orgasm, and produce that definitively human institution so rare among primates—the monogamous family. For Morris the male attraction to rounded buttocks, to smooth hemispheres of flesh, is inborn and may be the "key female Gender Signal for the human species,"[8] effective whether it appears in its original form, as breasts pushed up by a bra, or even as the rounded surfaces of a woman hugging her bare knees. Human buttocks do not swell on a periodic basis but are always protuberant in women (and men); sexually selected, buttocks may be one of humanity's oldest distinguishing and lust-engendering traits. The lack of human body hair (our status as "naked apes") Morris traces to the sensitivity of skin and its importance in erotic petting—another bonding mechanism crucial in the sex-mediated switch from furry rear-entry beasts to mature, communicating humans.

Although Morris's book opened up an entire discourse on human sexual evolution, his theories are problematic. Since monogamous mammals such as foxes and gibbons remain as couples for long periods during which they engage in no sexual activity at all, why should our ancestors have required heavy petting in order to "bond"? Nor is the "missionary position" necessarily a key to the formation of civilized humankind: bonobo or pygmy chimpanzees indulge in face-to-face sexual intercourse in the absence of either religion or human-style families. In fact, Morris has overlooked one major point: far from being a lure, womanly breasts might initially have been quite sexually unappealing to our male primate ancestors. Ancestral males would have avoided females lacking swollen vulvas and bright pigmentation. And they would have stayed away from the breasts with milk that indicated pregnancy and infertility; far from being aroused, they should have been repulsed by the sight of swollen mammaries.

Flat-chested nonhuman primates, including chimps, gorillas, and orangs develop bosoms only during lactation; their
breasts flatten soon afterward. Chimp females producing milk
are ignored by males. Estrous chimp females with flat breasts,
by contrast, are pursued by many different males and mate
frequently with a variety of them. The development of breasts
thus poses an evolutionary problem. Since nursing women
conceive less readily and tend to be less concerned with attracting males than caring for their own children, large-
breasted females are no more expected to be pursued by primeval males than judges at a beauty pageant to crown a pregnant teen. Yet the attraction of ample breasts inspires some
men to admiration, gawking, and the composition of lewd
limericks; it has even induced women to procure silicone im-
plants in an attempt to become more attractive.

The simplistic evolutionary explanation is that large breasts
signify a healthy potential mother, a good nourisher of infants.
In the Renaissance, as in the paintings of Rubens or Botticelli,
plump women were deemed the epitome of beauty. Another
clue to an older idea of female beauty are the prehistoric
figurines of rotund women, part of the evidence leading ar-
cheologists to believe that a generating Earth goddess was
widely revered before the dawn of patriarchal civilizations.
Once females began developing permanent breasts after puberty, whether or not they were nursing, the way was open
for men to consider them sexually attractive. They could even
have become, as Morris suggests, a striking example of bodily
self-mimicry, mirroring on the front the rounded, creviced
buttock signal to which males naturally respond. The slight
swelling of breasts prior to menstruation may even represent
a kind of anatomical hangover from a time when the breasts
increased in size during ovulation.

But that still leaves open the question, how did breasts *first*
become big? Originally they would have been *an*ovulatory
signs of infertility, as a woman's menstrual blood or pregnant
abdomen are still today. And human-style bloated breasts are
not even ideal for infants; some babies find it easier to drink
from and grip a skinnier, bottle-sized teat than a rounded,

slippery tit. The answer is that voluptuous breasts, like the absence of overt ovulation, may have lured dangerously jealous and sexually domineering ancestral adult males into a false sense of security. Such males would, if they could, totally restrict sexual access to their fertile females. But if the messages of her fertility were mixed, if she possessed breasts that captivated him even though they suggested she was no longer in heat, he would be distracted, less likely to monopolize her body during ovulation. "I propose the same function as discussed above for the evolution of concealed ovulation and continuous sexual receptivity, *i.e.*, to render additional ambiguity of female reproductive value in an imperfect system of female monogamy imposed by male domination," writes Smith.[9] Adding to an anatomy of deception that had begun with the loss of estrus and the spread of sexual interest beyond the circumscribed time frame of estrus, breasts remained swollen. Unable to figure out when an attractive woman was ovulating, an excited male had to pay much greater attention to her to ensure that she would bear his children and not someone else's; even prodigious adaptations for sperm competition would not have helped him if he was fundamentally uncertain as to the time of her ovulation. Females no longer ovulating or producing milk nonetheless displayed permanently enlarged breasts—breasts that, since they kept sexually jealous males guessing, prevented such males from devoting themselves to females only when they were in heat, and from abandoning them as soon as they became pregnant.

More primordial than gesture and speech is the semiosis—the system of signs—of the human body. And oppressed females could have countered male domination with subtle changes in physiognomy, evolving "devious" decoys, sending mixed messages in the medium of flesh. If Smith is correct, the wearing away of the meaning of one of the female body's ancient signs occurred in ancestral women. Like a worn coin passed so often that its date and value can no longer be read, the long-held, once-clear meaning of breasts wore down. For our simian ancestors breasts signified infertility, but with modern males the signification of breasts has altered and even reversed. During the time when breasts still connoted a lack of fertility, possessive males relaxed their vigilance over the activities of their ample-bosomed females. Such females were not completely unattractive to our male ancestors, and there may even have been reasons that made them, as we shall see, become more attractive over time.

In Smith's view, human promiscuity reached its height with the origin of *Homo erectus*, an ancestor who had begun to use fire and to hunt in groups. Female options were enhanced by cavorting with a number of males. Solitary males offered roaming females supplementary meat, and other foods, as solitary male chimps still do today. On the evolutionary logic that children conceived from romantic flings could well be their own, unpaired males devoted at least some of their resources to the children of unfaithful females. Dominant males in mixed-sex groups had difficulty guarding presumptive spouses; the trading of food in return for sexual favors may have been a matter—as prostitution still is today—not of morality but survival. Such primordial prostitution could have afforded females more food and superior living conditions for themselves and their children.

Fringe benefits accruing to females with deceptive breasts and secret ovulation were both genetic (escaping a possessive provider long enough to conceive a child with another, better male) and material (escaping possessive males to trade sex for goods with other males without necessarily becoming pregnant by them in the process). The immoral sound of the word "whore" is mainly the bias of a hypocritical and patriarchal social organization. Deceptive female anatomy gave females more choices and greater control over their reproducing bodies. But it did so by confusing males, who now, since they needed to commit themselves devotedly to a female if they wanted to have a good chance of being a father, were particularly vulnerable to infidelity. If breasts and cryptic ovulation evolved as ways of hiding fertility from the watchful eyes of men, so human society, largely in the hands of men, has countered by drafting laws to punish female infidelity: the treatment of marriage as a promise to "obey," greater social strictures on women relative to men to remain virginal and "pure," and laws more severe to the adulteress than the adulterer all smack of a male desire to reclaim control over female bodies—control that was lost during the evolution of the deceptive female form. "During recorded human history," Smith writes, "male attitudes forged by the potential for sperm competition have come to be reflected in political, legal, and social institutions that repress human females."[10]

Throughout many human cultures different values have arisen governing the social acceptability of promiscuity. Polygynous societies in which men have many wives are far more common than polyandrous ones in which a woman has more than a single husband. In parts of Nigeria where women have more than a single husband, the men who live in separate shelters probably are even more promiscuous than their wives. Cross-cultural surveys of human mating systems reveal that premarital and extramarital sex are always more prevalent in males, whereas adultery is more often and more severely punished when indulged in by females. (Thirty thousand to forty thousand Americans, for example—mostly Mormons in the state of Utah—live in polygyny.) In short, the double standard—in which promiscuous men are tolerated or even respected as "studs," whereas promiscuous women tend to be denigrated as "sluts"—is extremely widespread. The double standard is a reflection of male anger at the simple fact that maternity is certain, paternity is not. It, too, is perhaps part of the backlash against deceptive female anatomy by male-controlled societies.

In focusing on the "flowery combat" between the sexes it is easy to overlook its fruit: children. The story of men and women does not suffice; children are crucial to understanding the sexual evolution of human beings. The changeover from flat-chested estrous to nonestrous breasted females may have been helped along by the peculiarly impressionable psychology of young human beings. We must warn the reader that the psychological theory of imprinting we use here to explain the development of a liking for breasts fails to account nicely for psychological development of heterosexual females, who became attracted to breastless male bodies despite their early exposure to the mother. This weakness is, however, overcome if we assume that females are not as strongly sexually attracted to males as males are to them, and that women, embodying the original love object, are more narcissistic and sexually self-sufficient than men. In general, psychological theories seem to us less well established than evolutionary ones. Nonetheless, the sight of their nursing mothers may have so transfixed male toddlers that when they become adolescents they sought out similar women with bloated breasts who lacked any visible signs of estrus. In psychology the formative importance of early experience on later sexual development is generally conceded: a goal here is to recombine psychology and primate evolutionary biology into a plausible narrative.

Pillowtalk

A biological principle called "neoteny" enables us to understand many of the physical changes that took place as our apelike ancestors evolved to become the first humans. In neoteny, changes occur in which youthful characteristics—in humans, small jaws and large heads and eyes—are retained by adult members of a species. Neoteny is a delay in the life cycle's timing, a kind of retardational metamorphosis involving the genes or regulating circuits that govern the developmental timetable of the entire growing organism. The evolutionist Stephen Jay Gould shows neoteny at work in the history of cartoons: from a small-headed rat, Mickey Mouse changed into a more lovable figure, in large part because he was gradually given a proportionately larger head and bigger eyes. Gould argues that the later Mickey has been more successful for Disney Industries because he is more like a neotenous human infant—more vulnerable and therefore cuter.

Human infants enter the sound- and vision-rich environment of the jungle, savannah, or city at a stage in development when most mammals, still cozy and unaware, float in the white noise of the womb. Nonetheless, humans, endangered as infants by neoteny and the helpless state it confers, are also given opportunities they would never receive were it not for their premature entry into a perilous world.

All mammal infants are born with less hair than their parents: along with other signal traits of our species, the relative hairlessness of humans compared with apes may derive from neoteny. Nearly hairless at birth, humans were born more naked than they died. Their sensitive skin exposed to the elements, early humans took refuge by donning animal pelts, dressing in versions of the skins they had lost. They made themselves up and over in their own lost image, especially as winds blew over glaciers on tribes now well out of Africa. The transition to naked human apes entailed many neotenous changes. Remarkably, humans resemble young apes much more than ape adults: not only naked skin, but braininess, small jaws, and small canine teeth result from relatively minor changes in the regulatory mechanisms of embryonic development. Neoteny in the ancestral human line provides an explanation, in one fell swoop, for many of the physical—and psychological—differences between people and the other great ape members of our clan. And the physical disadvantages were made up for by the immense psychological advantage of being born in a premature state in which the capacities for learning and play were greatly expanded.

Our neotenous heritage surfaces in the response not only of parents but of lovers and children to babies; we react with an urge to care for childlike features such as big eyes, soft heads, and high-pitched voices. Defenselessness awakens in us nurturing desires. The human brain, according to the "triune brain" perspective of Paul D. MacLean, shares a vestige with all living mammals that is inexorably attuned to filial tenderness, religious and scientific awe, and other typically "mammalian" emotions.[11] The cry of a newborn is remarkably distressing. At some innate level, infants seem to inveigle us into picking them up, feeding, caring for them. Indeed, men may mimic little boys and women behave like small girls in order to evoke the cuteness to which the other gender unthinkingly responds. Freud noted that lovers develop a kind of debilitating dependency; the lover and beloved sink into a relationship marked by the helplessness of the one that is indissociable from the loving care of the other.

The nurturing desire is so strong that our parental side is stimulated by cartoon characters and stuffed animals. Ancestral kittens were carried by adoring humans to many continents: by raft, canoe, steamship, or airplane cats must have been transported, since no domestic cat can swim. Originally cats may have been domesticated because their meows mimicked the cries of our infants. People selected cuddliness and furriness in cats along with their usefulness to hunt rats and mice. Cuteness and snuggling is not only female or human; these propensities emerge from our mammalian heritage. Indeed, citing the deep and varied involvement of many father monkeys with their offspring, the feminist sociobiologist Hrdy wonders "whether the extraordinary capacity of male primates to look out for the fates of infants did not in some way pre-adapt members of this order for the sort of close, long-term relationships between males and females that, under some ecological circumstances, leads to monogamy."[12] Father–child bonds, in other words, may have been a prerequisite, and not the result of the father–mother–child bonds of human families.

First Impressions

Neoteny postpones, prolongs, and delays development. But the delay brings about psychological precociousness. "Prematuration"—to use the psychoanalytic term—exposes infants to the rich stimuli of the outside world at a crucial time in the development of their brains. Neotenous infants were held up to overpowering images—often of their mother's breast, her gaze, and childbearing hips—before they could even hold up their own heads or roll their little bodies over. The mother here is not even a "she," but an "it," an alien multilimbed goddess, an incomprehensible concatenation of body parts, of blissful nurturance, and terrifying rejection. Such fragmented images of the human body from early childhood may have an enduring effect within the psyche. For Jacques Lacan the disjuncture between the infant's disembodied perspective—its view of parts of itself and its mother in relation to its retrospective realization that the human body makes a whole—is so crucial that it overlays all adult experience. This jubilant, if illusory realization of wholeness by the infant Lacan refers to as "the mirror stage." The realm associated with it he calls "the imaginary." (An associated word is "imago," which Webster's Dictionary defines as "an idealized mental image of any person including the self.") In our evolutionary line, the early exposure of neotenous infants to bloated and nursing breasts may even have impressed or fixated images of these parts on infantile minds such that, later in life, when breasts were glimpsed, they were recognized as attractive and comforting—and perhaps even sexually stimulating. In his famous essay "the mirror stage"—of which, ironically, no original exists—Lacan mentions that gonadal development in a pigeon can be induced not only by another pigeon but by its viewing its own reflection in a looking glass. Experiments have shown that different species of gulls do not interbreed because their members have sexually imprinted upon the eyes of members of their own species. The herring gull, for example, which has yellow eyes and an orange eye ring, does not interbreed with the glaucous gull, which has yellow eyes and yellow rings; neither interbreed with Thayer's gull, which has a greenish iris and a purple eye ring. If nestlings are removed during the critical phase of sexual imprinting and placed in the nest of another species of gull, they will attempt unsuccessfully to mate with members of the foster species upon reaching maturity. Painting the eye rings of adults creates similar reproductive confusion.

Psychologists and psychoanalysts have discovered the lasting importance of the first five years of life. During these first five years one learns to feed oneself, to walk, and to control the urinary and anal sphincters. Children become fascinated with sexual differences, the presence and pride of place of penises in our male-dominated society, the ownership of body parts, the goings-on of parents. During these first years they speak: signifying, replacing, and supplementing what is longed for with the social pacifier of language. The speechless red-faced rage, the open-mouthed, fist-clenched tantrums of infancy give way to the resignation and relative calm of words. Speech entails mouth movements, the kind of self-satisfied lip smacking and questful touching of tongue to palate that, if it is not as delicious as food or as sweet and comforting as a stream of fresh breast-squeezed milk, is at least more social than thumb sucking. For the naturally handicapped human infant, far more able to perceive than to move, crying and speech are crucial to survival.

Leather, Lace, and the Fetish for Flesh

A founder of the so-called object-relations school, Melanie Klein, the British psychoanalyst, focused her attention on the earliest years of life. She revised Freud, moving the time of deepest impressions up to the first months of life. In extensive studies of children, she asserted that a version of the Oedipus complex—jealous hatred of the father and a desire to merge with the mother—is already detectable within the first year. The most critical psychic events for Klein, events involved in the formation of borderline personalities, adult neuroses, and paranoid schizophrenia, unfold for the infant during its first two months outside the womb. During its first month the baby's eyes, unable to focus, perceive its mother's presence uncertainly, through a mental kaleidoscope. These synecdoches, these "part-objects" of Klein, are crucial, if fragmentary perceptions. Unstable images and scents lead the infant to assign value to its mother's breasts: as its mother promises and revokes, behaves lovingly or persecutes, the breasts are "good" or "bad." As the eyes begin to focus, as early as the second month, the infant realizes that the bad breast for which it felt hatred and the warm beloved breast are one and the same. If in its fantasy life the infant fails to undertake the depressing and difficult task of forgiving the wicked mother and merging her with the good mamma, it may sacrifice its entire future psychic development. Klein's unique forms of therapy through carefully chosen play material yielded a high rate of success; in the wake of this success, Freud revised his view that the most important age for psychic formation was three to five years to earlier in life.

The events of early childhood are also thought to deeply influence later sexual development. Freud and his followers tended to stress the lability or plasticity of the sex drive—its amazing ability to be diverted in its direction like a misaddressed letter or an arrow plucked up by an eagle. Although Freud proposed that sex drive may be satisfied in a roundabout, sublimated manner, some American psychologists, influenced by behaviorism, locate the genesis and aims of the sex drive with daring exactitude. According to some, sexual orientation itself, either hetero- or homosexual, may be fixed by experiences that occur when a child is about three years old. The first love object for both boys and girls is a female—the mother—with her high voice, breasts, vulva, and other characteristics. Both sexes probably first "imprint" upon the mother but girls must modify their first attraction to women if they are to become heterosexual. "Imprinting" is image formation of an imperfectly symbolizing animal who looks for short-cuts, clues, and indices in the search for accurate information about the behavioral necessities for survival.

Glen Wilson, no Freudian but a psychologist familiar with animal behavior, suggests that sexual fetishes occur when the normal biological mechanisms of early childhood do not function properly. A young boy must "imprint upon" the sight of a woman's pubic area if he is to develop normally in later life. Indeed, libidinous attachments to shoes (easily seen from the eye-level of a child), undergarments, and wet, shiny, or furry material (reminiscent of a woman's pubis) may be the result of "errors" in brain mechanisms whose evolutionary heritage is to ensure the recognition by immature animals of the objects of their future—their mature—sexual desires. Although suggestive, an indication of the incompleteness of this notion of sexual imprinting can be seen in its inability to explain the development of young women. Following the logic of the theory, girls also would be expected to imprint upon their mothers, in which case they would grow up with a sexual predilection for women. Since most women are not lesbians, however, if we do not want to abandon the theory we must assume that sexual imprinting functions differently in males and females. Or, perhaps, as conventional psychoanalysis suggests, that the first love object of both males and females is indeed the mother—and that the special difficulty of becoming a heterosexual woman consists in making the switch to a love object of the opposite gender.

Such "imprinting" in action was demonstrated in famous experiments by the Nobel Prize-winning ethologist Konrad Lorenz. Removing the natural mother from ducklings and goslings on his estate in the German countryside, Lorenz exposed them to his own form instead. The animals, provided with the "wrong" stimulus, swam after Lorenz through the water and waddled behind him on the ground. Just as in parental imprinting the ducklings must be exposed to the mother bird, so in sexual imprinting, psychologist Wilson claims a crucial time exists during which little boys must be exposed to the evolutionarily proper sexual "target"—namely the sight of female genitalia. If a woman's pudendum is not seen, Wilson theorizes, boys may substitute feet, shoes, or frilly underwear. Lacy lingerie, or rubber, may "imprint" sexually upon the toddler's mind in the absence of exposure to a fully naked woman.

Although males of some species of fish and water fowl are known to mate with females of other species, in all animals males and females usually recognize and mate only with members of their own. They enjoy sufficient sexual intercourse enough times for continued propagation of the population. Any general failure to ensure mate recognition destines a species for rapid extinction. In sexually reproducing mammal species, the genes effectively delegate the responsibility of mate recognition to the brain. But the brain is even more complex and prone to failure than the genes; it may make mistakes, "misrecognize." Such errors in association prohibit individuals from reproducing.

The best explanation of human rubber fetishism, of an attachment to the look, feel, and smell of rubber, as opposed to sexual stimulation by the touch of flesh, is that rubber-love results from psychological malfunction in child development. Sexual attraction to rubber is inappropriate to the biological task of reproduction. Since rubber was synthesized for the first time only in recent centuries, a sexual craving of men and women for rubber could not have appeared before then. Rubber fetishism, Wilson infers, must develop through cues received within an individual's own lifetime.[13]

A more common fetish is leather, which as cowhide, shoes, saddles, and jackets, has been in use by our species for far longer than rubber. Leather also would have been viewed, smelled, and touched more often than rubber by children in milk-drinking, cattle-herding societies. From the sacred cow of India to the holster of a gunslinger, cattle have been part of our species development. The general liking for leather is not that different from the fetishizing of leather in a dominant/submissive sexual relationship. In both cases there is something slightly bestial—as if our long relationship with cows has tainted us with their image no less than the early exposure of goslings to Lorenz infatuated them with his. And, indeed, although errant and perverse, the gosling fetish for Lorenz, like the human fetish for leather may turn out useful—in the case of the goslings, by giving them a scientist to rely on in the absence of their real mother; in the case of leather fetishists, by solidifying human ties to cattle in herding societies fed by cowboy staples such as milk, butter, cheese, and steak.

In the language of artificial intelligence the sensory system of the fetishist has been "misprogrammed." But in the natural course of evolution such errors are normal. The course taken as a sexually reproducing species gives rise to another sexually reproducing species is itself errant. The sex drive's objects in thinking animals are not totally implanted and preprogrammed from birth but rather determined by environmental encounters; chance in the life of the individual, or history in the life of the species may radically alter them.

Chimps usually nurse for at least three years. Like chimps, the mothers of neotenous ape-children may have nursed their babies for at least three years. The physical features of their mothers—at the very time these mothers were swollen with milk and functionally infertile—would be crucial for psychic formation. Impressionable neotenous babies became adolescents and men; imprinted with the image of their milking mothers, they might have sought out mates with swollen breasts. Having "imprinted" upon lactating women, some would have preferred swollen breasts to swollen vulvas or other signs of fertility. This misreading of reproductive symbolism may have crucially affected the emergence of the human body. All humankind may be the offspring of sexual deviants—fetishists not of rubber but of nursing breasts.

This droll, slightly perverse thought reminds us that nature has no fixed morality. Over evolutionary time what is abnormal becomes normal, and vice versa. As an aside, incest also must have been important to evolutionary development. Without some bare modicum of inbreeding new sexually reproducing mammals could not evolve at all: animal species by definition require populations, groups of animals living in the same place at the same time; to be a species the members of a group must be able to interbreed to produce viable offspring. The sexual partners of any species appear to be weird deviants from the viewpoint of their descendants with whom they can no longer mate to produce viable offspring. Will the descendants of humans be as embarrassed by, and unattracted to their human ancestors, as we are by our ape heritage?

Females with swollen breasts who lacked estrus would have enjoined males to share in the upbringing of their neotenous children. If some sort of imprinting mechanism acted powerfully enough, then the most attractive females became non-lactators who still bore traits of lactation but were still ovulating; some apemen must have found protowomen—females with breasts and covert estrus—to be their heart's desire. Our ancestors at some point became so inbred that no other self-respecting anthropoids would lust after them any longer. Breasts and a new pubic modesty—the very subtleties that had made it impossible for male hominids to completely control the sex lives of female ancestors—now became sought after as distinguishing marks of the feminine, the very charms of women.

The Hymen

The last feature of women we wish to explore is the hymen. If breasts and the disappearance of estrus represent effective camouflage for the female in the battle of the sexes, the hymen may represent a victory for male reproductive interests. In his groundbreaking synthesis on the evolution of human sexuality, Smith calls the hymen "one of the great unsolved mysteries of human anatomy."[14] Smith, of course, may be mistaken; perhaps the hymen, like the clitoris or like meiosis, is simply a vestige, with no "purpose" or "meaning."

Since chimps, gorillas, and orangutans show no evidence of structures analogous to the hymen, we assume this structure evolved in the hominid ancestors to humans between four million and forty thousand years ago—after our line diverged from that of apes. The genesis of the hymen was perhaps a minor birth defect like webbed fingers or toes. A usually crescent-shaped flap of circular membrane partially blocking the entrance to the vagina, the hymen is more useless than an appendix or tonsils; indeed, if intact it is invariably ruptured with some pain and bleeding during a woman's first experience of sexual intercourse. Like the tearful crying of an adult, also unique to our species, the hymen's physiological function, if any, is obscure. Yet within the evolving text of the body it may be a sign: the hymen may have been selected for by those jealous and possessive men who wished to ensure against sexual betrayal.

Certain fishes and insects undergo genital "trauma"—tearing of the genitalia—and this behavior evolutionists have interpreted as a way, cruel though it is, of barring access to subsequent would-be fertilizers; like burning a bridge, the selfish males prevent others from following them into the coveted territory. The hymen works in reverse, ensuring fidelity prior to, rather than after, sexual intercourse. The intact hymen is perfectly correlated with the lack of pregnancy, although, of course, once deflowered, a woman may become pregnant by someone other than her boyfriend or spouse. For an early man uneasily reconciled to monogamy, an intact hymen may have assured him that a woman could be successfully impregnated by his sperm. The hymen, like the breasts, would be a carnal signifier, a body part with meaning, referring to something beyond its own mere presence.

The hymen marks the virgin. Virginity signifies a lack of previous infidelity, adultery, cuckoldry. Studies of people ranging from the Yanomamo of the Venezuelan jungle to midwesterners in the United States show that about 10 percent of men who presume they are the fathers in fact are not.[15] Perhaps our ancestors included muscular and intimidating polygynous males who would protect or feed only young females whose hymens bore testimony of their premarital chastity. A wealthy male who provides for several women is even more at risk of cuckoldry than a husband with only one wife. An australopithecine apeman or early human rich and powerful enough to obtain many wives increased his chances of fatherhood by choosing only virgins. Even in the United States today, a poor pregnant urban schoolgirl often names as father the most attractive or the best provider.[16] This strategy, which transmits the women's genes while curtailing the newlywed male's access to maximal siring, is an example of exploitation by females which the genetically clever male precludes when he agrees to devote his energies and abilities only to a woman who proves her virginity with the symbolic flesh of an intact hymen. The role of the hymen is therefore similar to that of the castrated eunuch who guards a haremful of concubines. There has been a long history of male distrust of the difficult-to-read female form; within this history both eunuch and intact hymen have been used to ensure the highest possible sexual fidelity. Perhaps it is no accident that in French the word *hymen* also has an older sense meaning marriage, matrimony.

If monogamy from the male vantage point is only begrudgingly accepted as a way of dealing with the cuckoldry always possible under the female body's cunning tactics of secret ovulation, continuous sexual receptivity, and breasts, then clever males may have recovered some ground in the battle for polygyny by using the hymen as a kind of congenital chastity belt or "seal of approval" designating that they have not—at least, not yet—been cuckolded. By providing only for the young bride whose hymen he has broken himself, our male ancestor augmented the odds that his genes were represented in successive generations. The daughters of the mother with a hymen would also have tended to have hymens and thus men could have perpetuated sexual selection for virgins with hymens until almost all little girls were born with the little membrane.

In only several generations, the hymen, fixed on by sometimes brutally jealous males as a transparent and unequivocal indicator of virginity, could have become established in the earliest human families.

Neon Jungle

We have assumed that the primate ancestors to women once advertised their fertility by colorful swellings but that they lost this estrus and developed breasts, thereby eluding stronger exploitative males whose interests were narrowly focused only on mating. Nonetheless, people may be still psychologically attuned to primate signs of amenability to coitus;

for clothing allows women, if and when they desire, to *mimic* estrus.

"The essence of all science lies in the philosophy of clothes," wrote Edward Nobles in a poem in the erotic publication *Yellow Silk*.[17] People may begin life as vulnerable infants but when undergoing puberty, the young adult emerges more beastly, physically—and perhaps mentally—more like an ape. The adolescent loses touch with what is perhaps most human: his or her nakedness, childlike openness, and exposed innocence. Pubic and underarm hair bring the youth closer to the physical appearance of wilder mammals; often enough a new interest in dressing fashionably, in appearing sexually desirable, coincides with the shaky human entry into adulthood.

Baboons (monkeys, not apes) have an estrus still more colorful than that of chimpanzees. Male baboons bare their fangs as they fight over estrous females with the same sort of jealous violence that sometimes afflicts men fighting in bars. Darwin admitted that "no case interested and perplexed me so much as the brightly-colored hinder ends and adjoining parts of certain monkeys. . . . It seems to me . . . probable that the bright colors, whether on the face or hinder end, or, as in the mandrill, on both, serve as a sexual ornament and attraction." Might not the sexiness of color from makeup to clothes come from a primate love of flowers and fruits? Evolutionary biologist Nancy Burley has shown, much to the chagrin and surprise of many of those who study them, that striped finches are so fond of the red skin that marks their species that they preferentially mate even with birds whose legs have become orange artificially by the placement of scientific identification tags. With their bright colors and alluring scents, plants attract mammals and birds who in roaming and eating them naturally disseminate their seed. Girls' names such as Rose, Daisy, Lily, and Iris suggest that females are allied to colorful flowering plants in the popular imagination. Bright colors one associates with the sweetness and intoxication of sexual love. Almost all the forest-dwelling "species of the genera *Cercopithecus* have elaborate patterns and colors of fur and skin on the face and body, involving brightly-tinted moustaches and beards and bibs and crests of hair," writes primatologist Linda Marie Fedigan. "Some species even have a great colored patch in the middle of the face, looking for all the world like the exaggerated painted nose of a circus clown."[18] Is the human use of makeup, hair color, tinted contact lenses, and God-knows-what future fashions a manifestation of the same primate love for ornamentation that has produced the sexually selected Mardi Gras faces of these simians?

We assume that foremothers once had periodically colorful labial and buttock swellings but somehow lost them. That with the universal adoption of clothing—including the "clothing" of permanently protubertant breasts—the loss of estrus was transported from body to mind, from the physiology of females cyclically coming into heat to the consciousness of women choosing when they wanted to be most attractive. Indeed, there is even an eerie similarity between the swelling and brightening of the lower parts of estrous monkeys and the clinging Day-Glo hot pink pants of a streetcorner prostitute, her behind slightly lifted, not momentarily as when the estrous chimp entices males to mount her, but all night long by her leather stiletto pumps. Perhaps we are wrong. Perhaps estrus has not completely vanished. It is as if, in those disturbing urban jungles called red-light districts, the ghost of estrus stubbornly remains.

4

LIZARD
TWISTS

To attempt to get at the foundations is to try to recover consciousness about things that have passed into the unconscious
stage; it is pretty sure to disturb and derange those who try it
on too much.

—SAMUEL BUTLER[1]

*Now a primate with a faintly chimplike face, black irises, claws, and
a tail, the once human dancer whirls across the floor, transforming
into a hissing green reptile—with an intelligent, if vicious expression.*

Lizard Love

Beneath the evolutionary stripper's naked human
skin lie the furs of an anthropoid ape. Under that primate's
coat lies a series of extinct forest-dwelling mammals, beings
that remain in part reptilian. Indeed, the reptilian sexuality of
our Paleozoic ancestors may persist subliminally in the human
mind. It is for this reason that we look to the instinctual patterns
of response in reptiles, specifically lizards and lizardlike reptiles, for clues to "primitive," biologically rooted, aspects of
human sexual behavior.

Although often neglected by students of animal behavior, reptiles as the evolutionary predecessors of mammals are more related to humans than the birds and fish more commonly discussed in the zoological literature. The diverse group of extinct reptiles that evolved into mammals are called synapsids. Among the reptiles, most of which no longer exist, living lizards are most like extinct synapsids. The silent, hieroglyphiclike "thought" of the ritualistic brains of these lizards—assuming that we can become privy to it—illuminates us as well as them. Yet the story of how people are lizardlike—still mentally part reptilian—should not be taken for granted simply because it has a scientific, anatomical basis. We should not assume that just because there is evidence that we retain reptilian traits, and that these traits are very old, that we cannot therefore change them. The terrible problem of the "horrified spectator"—being mesmerized by acts that seem alien but are our own, acts that are regretted by one part of us even as they are committed by "another"—crystallizes in the scientific notion of an archaic brain. We must be careful to remember here, as elsewhere, that scientific stories have their mythical elements.

One twisted tale of lizard sexuality elucidates our presumed reptilian inheritance. Some whiptail lizard species from the southwestern regions of the United States reproduce sexually; the populations of others, such as *Cnemidophorus uniparens*, comprise only females, uniparental, parthenogenetic creatures that belong to a spermless, all-female society. Females, however, go through the motions of making love: some females, behaving like males, mount fertile females, who then lay clutches of eggs. Since *Cnemidophorus uniparens* populations boast no males, the lizards never partake of heterosexual intercourse; nonetheless, the females, virgins till death, are no herpetological puritans. They "pseudocopulate." With arched back and looped tail one bites another's neck in the same ring-shaped posture assumed by males and females of related, heterosexual species. These imitations of heterosexual intercourse seem to help reproduction: pseudocopulating females lay three times as many eggs as their sexually inactive sisters over the course of the breeding season.[2] Such pseudocopulation appears to be under hormonal control, part of the altered reproductive pattern of a species that has evolved beyond sexual reproduction but not beyond sex.

Studies have revealed that all *Cnemidophorus uniparens* females are probably the progeny of a single hybrid mother. As a donkey and a horse can mate to produce a sterile mule, members of two different species of lizards sometimes mate to produce a genetically distinct individual. Unlike mules, however, the mother of this all-female species continued to have lizard babies without mating: chromosome and gene studies could not identify the male ancestor, but the maternal ancestor of *Cnemidophorus uniparens* was found to be, using the techniques of molecular biology, a female of the two-sexed whiptail species *C. inornatus*.

Looking at the ancestral two-sexed species helps explain how malelike mating behavior can remain even after the disappearance of the male gender. Mating begins in *Cnemidophorus inornatus* when the male, approaching the female, probes her body with his tongue. If she is willing he bites her on either the neck or the foreleg. Mounting her, he scratches her sides with his hindlegs, pushing her against the ground. Then he works his tail underneath her, bringing his cloaca into contact with hers. (The cloaca, which stores both excretory waste and sex cells, is an organ connected to the genitalia and the kidneys—a kind of bladder-colon-uterus in females and bladder-colon-sperm sac in males.) Below the cloaca, the *Cnemidophorus* male has two penises. He inserts one of his two paired penises (hemipenes) and penetrates her. He then releases his neck bite and twists his body into a donut shape, clamping his jaw upon the female's pelvic region. In this contorted position he ejaculates. Fascinatingly, in *Cnemidophorus uniparens*, the one-gender species, "mating" proceeds almost identically. The O-shaped contorted posture is assumed, but without either hemipene penetration or ejaculation. It is pure sexual posturing, in which one of the females convincingly assumes the role of a male.

In the all-female species, malelike mounting behavior is

triggered by the female steroid hormone progesterone. Herpetologist David Crews suggests that progesterone binds to a place in the brain that in the ancestral two-sexed species was reserved for the male hormone androgen.[3] But this androgen, a male hormone, is lacking in the all-female *Cnemidophorus uniparens* lizards. Thus it appears that female progesterone-binding proteins attach to a part of the brain called the anterior hypothalamus-preoptic area, acting to replace androgen and retain male behavior even in the absence of males.

If such sexuality were to appear in humans it might be like that portrayed fictionally in *The Left Hand of Darkness*, a tale woven around an inspirational sentence, "The King was pregnant," that came to Ursula Le Guin before she began to write. In Le Guin's award-winning novel, humanlike neuters on a planet called Winter periodically go into "kemmer"—a physiological transformation—at which time they become male or female.[4] Although people are not neuters reversibly subject to hormone-induced gender changes, human behavior, physiology, and even body traits are extraordinarily sensitive to tiny changes in the amounts or types of steroid sex hormones. Transsexuals, people who are surgically and hormonally treated in order to change sexes, do not consider their changes to be superficial; in contrast with the female impersonator or masculine lesbian, they believe their sex switch to be authentic. Hormones may make us irrational or moody, sexually aroused or unreceptive; presumably they trigger impatience, anger, and even jealous violence. Such a propensity for hormone-mediated changes not only in the body but in perception and behavior, deeply embedded in the sex lives of our predecessors, reaches beyond the roots of the human into our ancestral past.

However disconcerting to us today, sexual jealousy, same-gender violence, rape, and hierarchical obedience were keys to the survival of the prolific and diverse reptiles that, in the millions of years of the late Paleozoic era, preceded any mammals. Male bloodthirstiness, cunning, and a quickness to make and carry out threats worked to repulse other males. Other behaviors bonded reptiles into dangerous alliances capable of extinguishing rival groups. It would seem that at the level of the reptilian body-mind, sex and violence are in a strange concord. And yet to speak of the powerful existence of beastly modes of behavior—even of diabolical instincts—is not to declare that such behaviors merit approval because they led to the survival of our ancestors. It is rather to call attention to some of our apparently most deeply rooted traits—traits that must be recognized if they are to be altered.

Primordial Wings

One of the traits connected to the reptilian part of our brain is certainly posing or bluster: pretending to be more or other than we are. We share the reptilian part of the forebrain, called the R-complex for short, with reptiles and mammals. Experiments demonstrating the existence of this archaic part of the brain have been performed on modern animals ranging from lizards to squirrel monkeys. If one hemisphere of a portion of the forebrain of a green *Anolis* lizard is surgically impaired, and his eye is covered while the eye connected to the injured forebrain is left exposed to a rival lizard, the lizard sees his rival but makes no ritual display. But if the other eye is covered—leaving the healthy eye still connected to an intact R-complex—the male reacts with a species-typical challenge, a territorial display. The *Anolis* pushes up with his feet, swells out his throat fan, and changes his position to expose his imposing long side, his profile, to his male rival. He makes himself look *big*. Like a man obtaining a psychological advantage by puffing out his chest and holding up his head, the normal *Anolis* lizard with an undamaged R-complex behaves predictably "macho."

To the less than enlightened reptilian mind a part may appear as a whole. Enlarging the puffed-out throat fan or turning sidelong to expose a profile that occupies a big slice of the rival's field of vision is a form of protolinguistic deception. Potential enemies are frightened by display; indeed, they may be tricked into thinking that a huge animal, far larger than the one present, stands before them. Lizards today turn their profiles to each other—apparently to threaten and scare by seeming bigger than they are. Perhaps the typically American valorization of size, of big body parts, big houses, and big cars—the whole "bigger-is-better" mentality—manifests an archaic reptilian imperative still lurking in human brains.

To pretend to be big is impressive, but still more impressive is actually to be big. The dinosaur drama, culminating in extinction some sixty-five million years ago, is a story of gaining advantage by increasing in size. Is a craving for bigness encoded in the human R-complex? Translated into English, the dragonspeak of the R-complex might warn, *"Avoid animals bigger than me"* and *"Try to seem as big as you can."* "Feathered serpents"—the flying reptile *Archeopterix* and, more recently, giant nests replete with eggs belonging not to birds but to dinosaurs—have been discovered in the fossil record. Picturing the monstrous capacity for display of such beasts leads us to suggest a new hypothesis for the origin of wings.

If our scaly reptilian ancestors were entrenched in this trembling world of veiled threats and simulated size, birds—which some evolutionists argue are still so like dinosaurs they should be classified in the Dinosauria—may have originally evolved by playing tricks on the gullible reptilian mind. The evolution of birds has long been an enigma. Birds never evolved wings "in order" to fly; the first wings must have been mutant limbs fortuitously valuable for something other than flight. Some evolutionists suggest that birds used pre-wings and mutant feathery scales as insulation, a means of temperature control. But wouldn't the sudden expansion of winglike appendages used by birdlike reptiles also frighten their rivals? Might not the looming shadows have scared reptiles no less than a loud unexpected "boo" makes us jump back? The raising high of scaly wings, like the action of raising large banners bearing the image of a leader, was a premilitaristic display. The reptilian body-expanders would have deceived their enemies as to their true size. The wings-to-be would have cast large shadows, terrifying other animals in broad daylight. When suddenly lifted, pre-wings could have simulated the approach of much larger beasts. The use of such early wings would—like a rumbling vocalization by a small animal to mimic the ground tremors of a larger one or the car that suddenly backfires on a hot summer day—represent a violence that did not exist. Flightless, such wings would lie.

Snake Eyes

Fiction illustrates the conflicts caused by the part of the human forebrain we share with reptiles. The R-complex is so old and entrenched it overrides our better judgments, making us literally of two minds. The incarcerated protagonist of Walker Percy's novel Lancelot has amnesia but is gradually led by a priest or prison psychologist (it is not clear) to tell his story.[5] Lancelot's wife was unfaithful, his daughter's blood type does not match his own, his son is a homosexual, and he is disenchanted, to say the least, with the sexual revolution of the 1960s. A southerner, Lancelot longs for a time when disputes, as duels between gentlemen, were settled honorably. Instead, he obtains electronically distorted videotapes of his wife and daughter's promiscuous activities with members of a visiting film crew. Even as he kills his wife's lover with a Bowie knife Lancelot intellectualizes the event. It is as if the more recent, more mammalian and human portion of the brain, unable to control his R-complex, were making excuses for a horrible spectacle: ultimately jailed for murder, he compares the homicidal entrance of steel into arteries with the sexual entrance of the man's cells into those of his wife.

A more explicit appearance of the R-complex in fiction occurs in Snake-Eyes, a "cyberpunk" story set in the future. The hero, George, a human being whose reptilian brain has been electronically integrated into Aleph, a military computer, seems programmed as much by the former as the latter. In the company of a woman, he stares "into her dilated pupils, gold-flecked irises, clear whites, all signs so easy to recognize, so hard to understand: snake eyes."[6]

The retention of responses once crucial to survival but now positively endangering to the organisms in question is an example of "evolutionary drag." The taste for sugar and salt, gustatory responses that signaled important food sources in our animal ancestors, are mundane examples of evolutionary drag. The taste for them drags along after their usefulness has diminished. Salt maintains the internal chemistry of beings who evolved in saltier waters; sugars, an indispensable source of quick energy, were a rare treat in the jungle. Sugars signaled ripe fruit, important carbohydrates in ancient environments. But now, widely distributed around the world in refined forms, these substances are no longer in short supply; they are not sources of good nutrition.

The entrancing effects of bright colors in motion may derive from our pre-ape history as arboreal mammals and their reptilian ancestors, for whom brightly colored succulent plants were a key resource. We eat salted snacks and artificially colored confections, and children, intoxicated by inocuous plastic toys, stare hypnotically at the colors of a color television screen. Percy's Lancelot, yielding to emotions of extreme incivility, demonstrates the more sinister evolutionary drag of the reptilian brain. "Crimes of passion" were genetically rewarded in prehuman times insofar as they eliminated or curtailed the activities of sexual competitors. But despite its past genetic effectiveness, the reptilian heritage also works against itself: in jail in this late Holocene epoch (our modern geological age), a violent man such as Lancelot will sire few offspring. In our new world, where behaviors are legislated and their infractions punished, the unconscious techniques of ancestral survival become dangerous baggage. Although Lancelot realizes the harm he brings himself as he succumbs to jealous rage, he is powerless to resist it.

If jealousy, predatory viciousness, forced copulation, infanticide, and the homicidal behavior of troops and gangs sometimes increased the chances of survival of our reptilian ancestors, these behaviors may be hanging on powerfully owing to a kind of genetic momentum. It is possible that even rape—a heinous crime prevalent during wartime that all civilized persons will agree is never justified—was the most, if not the only, effective means of reproduction for certain men chronically excluded from other avenues of sexual intercourse and procreation. If so, then the impulse for violent insemination of women may have been reinforced when the children of rape victims inherited their fathers' dangerous tendencies.

According to John Alcock, the feminist hypothesis that rape is *solely* an instrument of social oppression against women— a violent means of male domination without biological basis— cannot be completely correct. Alcock points to the fact that raped women are not usually in positions of social power, but, rather, they are young, often poor, and relatively defenseless women in the peak of their childbearing years. If rape were mainly a cruel, oppressive social act, then older, more powerful women, he suggests, would be among the most likely targets. Alcock's thesis does not suggest that hatred of and violence toward women, perhaps stemming from the early domination of the child by the mother, is not also enacted during a rape. Perhaps women of childbearing age are most often raped because the mothers of rapists, perceived by the weak infant to be Godlike in their power, were also usually young women. Indeed, since children, old women, pregnant women, and men are also raped, it would be folly to claim that rape is *simply* a vestige of earlier, more brutal, less mammalian modes of animal reproduction. Nonetheless, the question lingers as to whether sexual violence is partially the result of the reptilian brain developing—or misdeveloping—in sexually arousable young people.

Squirrel Monkey's Mirror

The intact R-complex is involved in sociosexual behavior not only in reptiles but in intelligent primates. Squirrel monkeys, creatures far closer to our evolutionary lineage than extinct reptiles or *Anolis* lizards, communicate with their penises. Although they do not speak, squirrel monkeys communicate on a preverbal—"physiological"—level. This nonverbal, vocal, bodily, and chemical signaling is called "prosematic" by neurobiologist Paul MacLean. Figuring heavily in seduction and aggression, in dominance and submission, signaling by the prominent display of an erect penis was documented by MacLean. These monkeys show off their erections not only to indicate sexual desire, but to greet and to threaten. In one species of squirrel monkeys, males invariably raise their erection to their own reflections when seen in a mirror. Apparently squirrel monkeys doing this are recognizing or trying to frighten away what they perceive to be rivals. Because they predictably display to their image, MacLean studied the effects of brain ablations—careful removal of various portions of the brain—on the squirrel monkeys' behavior. MacLean found that the erection display was not connected to the mammalian cerebral cortex. Indeed, bilateral removal or destruction of the neomammalian and paleomammalian portions of the primate forebrain had little effect on erect penis display. Bilateral lesions of parts of the ancient reptilian R-complex, however, "short-circuited" the display. An "R-complex-impaired" squirrel monkey no longer exhibits his penis to his mirror image! MacLean was fascinated to find that, apart from not holding his penis up to the mirror, the postoperative squirrel monkey acted virtually normally.

Looking in the evolutionary mirror, monkeys—at least MacLean's squirrel monkeys—are seen to perform a particular ritual of sociosexual exhibitionism at the behest not of their mammalian mental faculties so much as of their R-complex. Tucked inside our brian, this R-complex, so similar to the generalized forebrain of turtles, lizards, and crocodiles, suggests that the sexual core of human behavior is still reptilian. However cultivated, orderly, and rational we act, a part of the brain stalks in the shadows like a poisonous, hissing, fork-tongued snake. (It is perhaps no accident that the worst insults, the most violent epithets contain swear words that also refer to sexual love; such double entendres seem to be second nature for the reptile within.) To this part of us, neither the theory of evolution, nor any other abstract concept, such as that even of time, makes real sense. It is even possible that our reptilian brain recognizes itself when we talk about it. Perhaps this anatomically and neurochemically distinct part of the brain even forms the material basis for the unconscious functions that Sigmund Freud called "primary processes." Although he parted company with biology to develop a distinct kind of discourse, Freud had always hoped that his speculations on mental functioning would someday be grounded in a knowledge of anatomy.

The Dragon Within

Mammals have not lost their reptilian heritage. It is virtually an evolutionary principle that no body part or chemistry once crucial to an ancestor is ever lost without a trace, although such features can be radically altered. Life is extraordinarily conservative; organisms embody their own histories. So it is that the typical forms of reptilian behavior may endure within human beings. Such forms include selection and preparation of homesite, establishment of territory, marking of territory (often by urine or defecation posts, showing place-preferences), and trail making. To defend territories reptiles ritualistically display their colored and adorned bodies. Some triumphantly assume distinctive postures or change colors to signal victory or surrender. And hordes of reptiles may partake of what herpetologists call isopraxis, imitation behavior. Marine iguanas, for example, move en masse to graze on the bottom of the ocean and then together they return to bask in the sun. Choruses of geckos and the vocalizations of crocodiles begin and end in concert. Turtles migrate in vast, dense, slow-moving queues. During spring, after emerging from hibernation dens, great numbers of snakes mate in large groups. Each female is found wound up in a "snake-ball" with her mate, the pair entwined in the characteristic copulation posture.

The turtles (Chelonia) are reptiles, although with their hard, head-hiding shells and slow pace, they have changed little since branching off from the stem reptiles, the prototypes not only for turtles, terrapins, and tortoises but for our direct ancestors, the synapsids or "mammallike" reptiles. Other stem reptiles evolved into dinosaurs and birds.

Although crowd behavior typifies the reptile, some individuality and personality have also been recorded. Rotumah, the century-old giant land tortoise from the Galapagos Islands died from "sexual overexcitation," wrote his monographer, Lord Walter Rothschild, in 1897.[7] Appparently after about 150 years of adult life, Rotumah could not bear separation from his lifelong sexual partner, who, two years earlier, had accidentally been left behind in Sydney, Australia. Certainly sexuality, as important for their reproduction as for ours, was and is a major focus for reptiles.

The largest living reptiles, with the species name *Varanus komodoensis*, are the Komodo "dragons" that inhabit the Lesser Sunda Islands in Indonesia. Weighing some 1350 kilograms (over 300 pounds), a Komodo may stretch as long as three meters. *Varanus* perhaps resembles the stem reptilian ancestors of mammals more closely than does any other living genus. The females bury their eggs in trenches from two to ten meters deep. The hatchlings live in trees. The dragons eat everything from insects to water buffaloes. They occasionally even ambush and stalk a live deer, but are content to eat the carcass. Sometimes they hiss.

The sex life of these monster reptiles is easy to observe. The Komodos apparently recognize each other and form faithful couples. Their sense of smell, unusually fine for reptiles, and partner recognition probably represent an advance in cognitive powers over their (and our) reptilian ancestors. Foreplay consists of much tongue flicking about the head and top of the hind legs; mating usually occurs conveniently close to feeding sites. Komodos, like alligators and crocodiles, can be vicious. Males mount males but this sexual posturing seems to signal

social superiority rather than reproductive prowess. Deep claw-
ing by a male of a female's neck and biting of the neck and
shoulder during mating were witnessed in heterosexual encounters. One study reports that a 2.3-meter-long female severely lacerated a 1.8-meter-long nonresident male when he
attempted to mount her. The female left for home but once
there her partner, an even larger male, chased her away from
their feeding site, as was his general practice.[8] Such anecdotes
indicate that the strange connection between sex and violence
may be a function of the status of both as ancient survival
needs, needs related by the greater simplicity of an earlier
evolved brain.

Serpentine Myths

The mythology of all human cultures proliferates
with reptiles, from Quetzlcoatl, the feathered serpent of the
Aztecs, to the Devil assuming the form of an evil serpent before
the expulsion of Adam and Eve from the Garden of Eden. A
biblical account depicts Moses tossing a long stick, which then
slithers away, a squiggling serpent. One of the forms in which
the Great Mother was worshipped was a snake. Among reptiles,
snakes especially seem to have assumed a symbolic role in
Western culture. Is the snake merely another Freudian phallic
symbol, or is it something more?

Unlike her immortal sisters, Medusa was a human, indeed,
a beautiful young woman pursued by many but yielding to
none, until she was wooed by Poseidon, god of the sea. But
by lying in a flowery field with Poseidon she enraged Athena,
who envied Medusa's beauty. As punishment, the goddess
turned Medusa's lovely locks into a seething mass of serpents
and made her face so ugly a mere peek at it would turn a
person to stone. Still enraged, Athena enlisted Perseus to cut
off Medusa's head. Athena saved Medusa's face to make an
aegis, a shield modeled after the thundercloud of Zeus, so

frighteningly effective that it paralyzed—like a startled lizard freezing in its tracks—those who dared to meet it with their gaze. The wound from Medusa's neck became the winged horse Pegasus and the drops of blood that drooled from Medusa's amputated neck onto the desert metamorphosed into poisonous serpents, sliding away across the sand.

For Freud the sight of snakes in the place of hair offers security to the onlooker who, startled at the woman's lack of external genitalia and hallucinating the site of an amputated penis, is comforted by the proliferation of serpentine phallic symbols at Medusa's head.

Are we simultaneously attracted and repulsed—frozen and fascinated by the reptilian spectacle—because of a dual legacy: the superimposition of the new mammalian mentality upon the old reptilian psychology? We evolved from the stem reptiles, which gave rise to the mammallike reptiles, the synapsids. Synapsid fossils are found on every continent including Antarctica, and these mammallike reptiles reached their heyday in Permian and Triassic times, from about 250 to 150 million years ago, before most dinosaurs had begun to evolve. After about 150 million years ago, however, the synapsid fossils disappear: it is thought that most of these mammallike, egg-laying forms were genocidally chased from their niches and eaten by thecodonts, the swift forerunners of the dinosaurs. So the stem reptiles branched off to become both dinosaurs and their mammal relatives; the reptilian descendancy includes not only Komodo dragons and dinosaurian monsters but the mammal forerunners they terrorized for tens of millions of years. The terror of giants such as *Brachiosaurus*, which weighed the equivalent of twelve African bull elephants, must have been so great that mammals in the vicinity of dangerous reptiles who failed to tremble and flee soon died, leaving no descendants.

Frequently video games, toys, comic strips, and television programs successfully feature the motif of the giant reptile. Children want the dinosaur monsters they fear to become their imaginary friends. And adults share in this ambivalent reckoning of the reptile. Aboriginal rock paintings from a western region of Australia depict women symbolically joined by what appears to be menstrual blood streaming between them as they dance. This same blood is redrawn as a coiled serpent. In the myth two serpent-entranced sisters first give names to things at the beginning of time. The two women, called the Wawilak sisters, take turns dancing, capturing the phallic snake's eye although both are quite tired. The sisters charm the python, called the "Rainbow Serpent," who, captivated by the smell of menstrual blood, turns distractedly from one to the other. Ultimately, in this aboriginal tale, as the younger Wawilak sister swayed from side to side, she began menstruating such that "the python, smelling more blood, came forward without hesitation."[9] The sisters, mutually menstruating, thus succeed by giving birth to the dangerous and unruly snake whose powers they fear.

Such myths contain a sexual element and yet their enchantment lies elsewhere, perhaps in the transformation of sexuality, perhaps in the theme not of slaying the awful dragon, hacking it apart, but of *taming* it, bringing the beast within the mammalian manifold. As in the famed East Indian trick of charming a snake with the notes of a flute so that it uncoils, reminiscent also of the trick in which a rope thrown into the sky becomes rigid and a boy climbs it, so in the ancient discipline of Kundalini yoga a cosmic and feminine energy is pictured as a sleeping serpent coiled at the base of the spine, slightly below the genitalia. As spiritual development occurs, the Kundalini flashes like a bolt of lightning upward through the *susumna*, a slender duct in the spinal cord that culminates in the brain. The result is a limp ("passive, cold, and lifeless") body and an enlightened brain: *samadhi*, a state of deathless rapture.[10] As the philosophy commentator and translator Walter Kaufman writes:

> One of the most remarkable features of the sex impulse is that it obviously has a physical basis but is capable of assimilating other needs and desires; for example, the desires for security, reassurance, and conquests, and the need to fill a frightening void. Desires and needs of this kind are often mistaken for sexual needs although they can be satisfied nonsexually.[11]

So, too, the symbolism of unleashing or harnessing the serpent within is undeniably sexual, and yet at the same time forms a mythological whole that cannot be reduced to a simple evolutionary explanation.

The beauty of myths may be precisely their kinship to dream. Like dreams, myths cannot be elaborated without loss of meaning: they are themselves irreducible, crystalline, more a narrative source of explanation than items to be explained. Perhaps that is why Freud leaned so heavily on the myths of Oedipus, Narcissus, upon dreams, and paleontological fables. These flowing tales twist at the heart of *logos*, logic; they are the seething mythological center underlying "scientific" explanation. Evolutionary stories, based on a linear conception of time, logically explaining present circumstances as the sequelae of past ones, are in particular convincing. Myths, by contrast, have a timeless quality. They are more honest in that they are less likely to be taken at face value. Suspended in time, all myths resemble the slippery uroboros, the ringing serpent that disappears into and is yet produced out of itself, the dream serpent that swallows its own "tale" in order to give birth to itself ever anew.

Synapsid Consciousness

By deducing brain size from the size of fossil skulls, UCLA professor Harry Jerison is one of the few scientists brave or foolhardy enough to have attempted to reconstruct the origins of consciousness. The preconditions for human language—"the measure of the complexity of the reality that *Homo sapiens* creates," as he says[12]—probably arose some seventy million years ago, long before people. Language, for Jerison, is the encoding of many, often simultaneous events into symbolic series, into stories.

By the end of the Permian period, some 245 million years ago, almost all mammallike reptiles died. Many may have been eaten by fast and ferocious cousins—thecodonts—forerunners to the dinosaurs. A few synapsids remained. Under the cloak of night these synapsids may have ventured out to feed on unattended reptile eggs and young. Like a blind man who develops an increased sensitivity to sound, our synapsid ancestors found their way around in the frightening dark. Indeed, those synapsids that survived appear to have switched from a reptilian perception dependent mainly on sight in the sunlit day to perception nearer to that of early mammals primarily dependent on sound in the obscurity of night.

Each animal species has its own characteristic perceptual world. The perceptual smell-world of a dog, for example, differs greatly from the colorful visual world of a bird, and from the ultraviolet light world of the honey bee fluttering between dazzling flower petals. A modern way of "thinking about the perceptual world," writes Jerison, "is as a construction of the nervous system designed to explain the sensory and motor information processed by the brain."[13] The work of the brain is consciousness, and consciousness involves untold, perhaps unstoppable "electrochemical" firings of nerve cells comprising neural networks.

> If a significant number of these events can be recoded as "objects" in "space" and "time" . . . the work of the brain as it processes its information will obviously be easier. . . . We may then assume that vertebrate species with less elaborate brains transform sensory information into motor neural information with little or no intervention of the kind of modeling implied by consciousness and the construction of perceptual worlds.

Vision in reptiles may be a sort of retinal reflex, a "reaction pattern" in which a specific impulse or stimulus leads each time to the same instinctual pattern of behavior. Reptiles and amphibians see but they do not see. If its eye is surgically rotated in its socket to produce inverted images the frog never adjusts to the upside-down visual space; the frog unsuccessfully attacks upward with his tongue to catch a fly on his foot. The frog's *Umwelt*—its sensory world—contrasts dramatically with our own: experiments equipping humans with special spectacles show that we only temporarily invert images of our surroundings. After persistent exposure the reversed image rights itself (though removal of the glasses necessitates a re-righting). Optical imagery is processed not merely with the eyes but with much of our brains. Among reptiles, however, "spatial representation is coded by an analyzer located in the retina itself."[14] In Jerison's reconstruction, mammals evolved from nocturnal reptiles. Whereas their reptile ancestors instinctively responded to visual stimuli, the new mammallike reptiles survived by listening.

The sonic tracking of predators was difficult at first. A series of scuffles in the dark had to be retained and integrated into a visionlike map of the predator's approach, the prey's escape. For nighttime hearing to replace daytime vision, "neural circuits had to translate temporally encoded patterns of auditory nerve impulses into the equivalent of the spatial 'maps' that had been generated more directly by the spatially distributed sensory elements of their reptilian ancestors' retinas."[15] But the maps were not the territory. To appreciate in reverse how difficult it was for our ancestors to use hearing rather than seeing in order to sense actions at a distance, try "hearing" a tune by staring at the squiggling patterns on the screen of a stereo oscilloscope. The immense difficulties of translating a temporal series of auditory "snapshots" into a reliable spatial "map" drove the enlargement in the auditory cortices of mammals, beginning in the late Triassic some 200 million years ago.

Major shifts occurred in ancestral perception, in Jerison's view. Mammallike hearing was the first. Nocturnal mammals retained the reptilian daylight visual system, which evolved into the mammalian rod system, "useful in twilight and moonlight as a crude distance sense for position and excellent one for the response to motion." More important, "The new role of hearing insured a neural representation of a time dimension with time intervals at least of the order of seconds available for 'time binding' temporally disparate events into a unitary stimulus for action."[16] Our ancestors began to distinguish objects in space and maintain awareness of them even when they turned their backs. The combined data now coming from a fine sense of hearing *and* a visual system allowed the position of objects located by sound to be confirmed by vision, and vice versa. The coexistence of reptilian retinal vision with early mammal audition integrated and synergized. The basis of naming and the nouns of language may ultimately derive from this merging of senses that allowed our ancestors to map their surroundings accurately, claims Jerison. Once mammallike audition developed, it would have been highly favorable to integrate the spatial map made from temporally held sounds with the visual stimuli coming in through the eyes. Those animals that merged their visual and auditory maps into a single audiovisual perceptual grid efficiently hunted, fought, and escaped. They left more descendants.

By seventy to sixty million years ago most species of giant, swift, and diurnal reptiles, including all the dinosaurs, had died. These dramatic late Cretaceous extinctions made room for the evolution of many new mammal species. Fine daytime color vision evolved; the cone-shaped cells, exquisitely sensitive to color and light, apparently evolved from the repatterning of mammalian retinal rod cells and their connections rather than from the old reptilian system. This was a wholesale mammalian brain revision. Reevolving sight became the basis of a new corticalized (inside-the-brain) vision. Other perceptual shifts followed. The encephalized auditory system that could bind temporally discrete sounds into charts of the surrounding space was exploited in vision. That is,

> in addition to its normal role in spatial mapping, mammalian vision would be time-binding, analogous to the way hearing can unify a complex sequence of tones into melodies. Like hearing, this new mammalian vision would be highly cephalized. . . . Visual images in such a system could be stored in some form for the order of seconds or longer and could maintain "constancy" under transformations in time and space.[17]

A further enhancement of auditory capabilities evolved in the "last million years or so. . . . The auditory system would . . . have the property of converting sounds and sound patterns into objects and producing yet further elaborations of the perceptual world, in particular with respect to time." Jerison rightly notes that the "quality of language that makes it special is less its role in social communication than its role in evoking cognitive imagery";[18] we should marvel, he says, that changing experience is interpreted as personal movement rather than a changing world observed by a fixed observer. Finally, the "threshold was reached for the evolution of perceptual worlds when 'time' became a central element in the system of analysis for distance information."[19] For Jerison, consciousness of time occurs for the first time in these early mammals who managed to reevolve vision after having developed a keen sense of hearing; the experience of time becomes the synthetic by-product of a new kind of audiovisual perception.

Throwing in Time

Beleaguered by journalists who had once again asked him to summarize his theory of relativity in a single sentence, Einstein admonished his admirers to accept his reply as sort of a joke. He explained that prior to his work everyone thought that if all of the matter were to be removed from the universe at least space and time would remain. Einstein, illustrating "relativity," stated that his contribution was to show that if matter were removed, space and time would disappear too. Similarly, we would like to suggest that time itself evolved in the course of human evolution. This statement is not meant simply as a joke but rather as a kind of koan or what in philosophy is called an aporia—an opening, an unavoidable contradiction, a point of (no) return.

Our species *Homo sapiens* would be better named *Homo seriatum*, claims neurobiologist William Calvin, because our distinguishing feature is that we narrate in series, we tell stories, we write in linear prose, and plan ahead.[20] Well, of course, since evolution is itself a story, our attempt to explain ourselves as the species that evolved to tell its own story is undeniably fraught with a certain mysterious circularity. Nonetheless, Calvin derives our human penchant for linearity from our ancestors' success in the Darwinian task of leaving many progeny: they developed powers of concentration and calculation, and acquired food largely by throwing rocks and other objects at game. Our ancestors plotted the trajectories of the stones and barbed, poisonous sticks they threw. The part of the brain involved in hitting moving targets, associated with right-handedness and specialization of the brain hemispheres, enlarged over evolutionary time as our ancestors became more accurate hurlers. Moreover, according to Calvin, the calculations involved in stunning small game with rocks made use of the same brain functions that became crucial for verbal logic. Individuals' success, over time, of throwing rocks (generally with the right hand), to kill rabbits, deer, and game birds, led to an adaptive increase in structures associated with throwing, which are also the site of language-related ability in the left brain. Calvin pictures young mothers holding their babies in their left arms close to their hearts in order to keep them quiet while they held projectile weapons in their right hand. Throwing meant aiming, aiming meant planning; through these acts arose the calculus of killing animals with stones. The increase in serial-processing abilities predisposed evolving humanity for foresight and anticipation; it was, Calvin believes, prerequisite not just for pitching baseballs but for the splendid *Homo sapiens* virtuosity, *language*.

The German philosopher G. W. F. Hegel distinguished between the knowledge of philosophy and that of science. *Richtigkeit*—correctness in the scientific sense —is not *Wahrheit*—truth in the artistic, philosophical, or aesthetic sense. Picasso, who asserted that each painting he created was a version of the truth, might be accused of lack of *Richtigkeit* in the portrayal in his painting *Guernica* of the events of the Spanish Civil War. The painting, from a scientific standpoint, is an abstraction; it is not photographic, and records no real events. And yet *Guernica* captures the spirit of the Spanish Civil War perhaps better than any documentary.

The narratives of Calvin and Jerison make scientific sense;

if not accurate they are at least plausible. But philosophically, the linear stories of these scientists, which purport to do nothing less than explain the origin of the human sense of time, sew things up a bit too neatly. Moving gently down the invisible seam of scientific texts such as these, discovering its texture— and here we search for *Wahrheit*, not *Richtigkeit*—a collossal rip in the patchwork must be confronted whenever mention is made, within the explanatory discourse of a *story*, of the *origin of linearity*. The story of how animals learned to perceive time is no ordinary story: it is the story *of* stories, the story that tells us where the sense of story-telling comes from, how it arose. And since story-telling in evolutionary discourse is always a form of explanation, the origin of time is already an explanation of explanatory power whose self-reference reminds us of that self-swallowing figure, the serpent uroboros. This is because evolutionary logic explains the present in terms of the past, but with the origin of the animal perception of time the foundation of this logic is located and, by implication, explained.

Conscious images often seem to come all at once, whereas linear order, logical development, is an imperative of science and its presentation, whether technical or popular. Agnes Arber, Cambridge University plant morphologist and member of the Royal Society, explains the "terminal stage in biological thinking." At the end of the line, at the end of inquiry's voyage "the biologist stands back from the individual jobs to which he has set his hand, in order to see them in the context of thought in general."[21] In a chapter entitled "The Biologist and the Written Word," the English botanist expunges any notion we may have that she is being vague or abstract merely out of ignorance:

> Another hindrance, not peculiar to science, is that, by the limiting convention both of tongue and pen, words can be placed only in simple linear sequence, temporal in speech, but translated into spatial order in writing. The experience of one's own thinking suggests that it moves, actually, in a reticulum (possibly of several dimensions), rather than along a single line. Even those who cannot accept the reticulum metaphor, might

agree that thinking is like a river, which includes eddies and still backwaters, though, considered as a whole, it progresses in one direction. Neither a reticulum nor a river can be symbolized adequately in a linear succession of words. A written account is a mere thread, spun artificially into a chain-like form, whereas, in the weft of thought from which it is derived, the elements are interconnected according to a more complex mode. Haller recognized this nearly two hundred years ago, when, in speaking of relationships within the monocotyledons, he said: "Nature has linked her kinds into a net, not into a chain; men are incapable of following anything but a chain, since they cannot express in words more than one thing at a time."[22]

Linear time—the time of books, of words—hampers us. Such time is distinct from the time of dreams or "the unconscious." There may be, that is, a "reptilian" kind of time. Aspects of dreams—including the distorted sense of time, predominance of imagery somehow related to sexuality, a surrealistic movement and a cinematic visuality—suggest they are related to reptilelike perception. Curiously, only mammals and birds—precisely the two classes of animals descended from the reptiles—need to dream. Reptiles do not dream, but their waking consciousness may be similar to our dreaming one.

Hostile to psychoanalysis because it is deemed "unscientific," some decry the psychoanalytic attempt to find meaning in dreams. For British biologist Peter B. Medawar, dreams are simply nonsense, and it is a mark of silliness, of a "gothic" love of mystery, to interpret them. "Those," he says, "who enjoy slopping around in the amniotic fluid should pause for a moment to entertain (perhaps only unconsciously in the first instance) the idea that the content of dreams may be totally devoid of 'meaning.' There should be no need to emphasize, in this century of radio sets and electronic devices, that many dreams may be assemblages of thought-elements that convey no information whatsoever: that they may just be *noise*."[23]

Medawar bitterly attacked psychoanalysis for its premature and pseudoscientific attempts to understand in psychological terms what are in his view more likely organic brain diseases such as schizophrenia. There is some truth in psychoanalysis as there was in mesmerism and in phrenology (for example, the concept of localisation of function in the brain). But, considered in its entirety, psychoanalysis won't do. It is an end-product, moreover, like a dinosaur or zeppelin; no better theory can ever be erected on its ruins, which will remain for ever one of the saddest and strangest of all landmarks in history of twentieth-century thought.[24]

Despite such harsh pronouncements, we think it ill-advised to *dismiss* psychoanalysis and philosophy as pseudoscientific, antiquated, or gothic.

For Nietzsche the world is metaphorical, beginning with the "first metaphor" of neuronal impressions becoming mental images. These mental images then become transferred into words, and so on, in a series of metaphorical transformations whose beginnings are difficult, if not impossible, to pinpoint, given our current state of knowledge of neurobiology and mental processes. Even if, wrote Nietzsche,

waking life is not as free as dream life, is less fictional, less unrestrained . . . our instincts, when we awake, likewise merely interpret our nerve stimuli and determine their "causes" in accordance with their requirements. There is no really essential difference between waking and dreaming. . . . Our moral judgements and valuations are only the images and fantasies of a physiological process unknown to us, a kind of convenient language to describe certain nerve stimuli. All our so-called consciousness is only a more or less fantastic commentary upon an unconscious text, one which is maybe unknowable but yet felt. . . . What are our experiences, then? Much *more* what we attribute to them than what they really are. Or should we go so far as to say that nothing is contained in them? To experience is to fictionalize.[25]

Hieroglyphic Dreaming

In an examination of Freudian and other writings, Jacques Derrida marshals evidence to show that dreams are in a strange sense hieroglyphic. They are rebuslike, mixing pictures and syllables, symbols and sounds, with a "grammar" peculiar to each dreamer. For example, in Egyptian hieroglyphics an eye denotes an eye, but it also denotes the first letter of the Egyptian word that means "eye." Meaning looks out to that which lies beyond itself. Dreams, writes Derrida, may be "constructed like a form of writing" and they "would only manipulate elements . . . contained into the storehouse of hieroglyphics, somewhat as written speech would draw on a written language."[26] Freud, according to Derrida, "doubtless conceives of the dream as a displacement similar to an original form of writing which puts words on stage without becoming subservient to them."[27] The images of dreams are seen by the moving but closed eyes of the dreamer.

Like an Egyptian hieroglyphic or Chinese ideogram the recognizable appearance of the dream image tends to obscure the importance of its multiple, and potentially very different, meanings, which are dependent upon context. Freud wrote: "My procedure is not so convenient as the popular decoding method which translates any given piece of a dream's content by a fixed key. I, on the contrary, am prepared to find that the same piece of content may conceal a different meaning when it occurs in various people or in various contexts."[28]

The Unsound

The emphasis on the visual rather than the verbal, on sight over sound, reflects the difference between reptilian and mammalian perception. Hearing, the auditory function retained in reptiles, is integral, less a whole-brain activity and less a necessity for survival than in mammals. Turtles, more sensitive to auditory cues than most reptiles, are nearly deaf to sounds in air. Rather, turtles put their heads down to the ground. They hear less through their ears than through their bones: sound is conducted through the "eardrum" of the turtle shell. Most living reptiles are also dumb. Geckos, a kind of

lizard, are the only known to have vocal cords. Members of
one species *(H. frenatus)*, especially the adult males, "chirp."
By passing air between their vocal cords, tensed and vibrating
at right angles to the airstream, geckos also "churr." And geckos
hiss, a noise they make by rubbing their tail scales against each
other. Another kind of lizard, chameleons, hiss when ap-
proached by predators; they have been reported to "bark" during encounters with members of their own species. According
to MacLean, "In the evolution of mammals, the development
of vocalization and hearing became of the utmost importance
for maintaining parent–offspring relationships under conditions of obfuscation."[29] Reconstructing prehistory from the fossil record of mammallike reptilian bones, MacLean notes that
"in the advanced forms, the quadrate and articular bones were
becoming smaller, but were far from being transformed, re-
spectively, into the incus and malleus of the mammalian inner
ear."[30] If the reptile still lives in a largely silent and mute realm
within the chatter of the speaking and conscious brain, it
appears to find its expression in ways that differ from traditional
hearing-oriented logic. The reptilian mind is, in a double
sense, *unsound*.

The French dramaturge Antonin Artaud's "theater of cruelty" was to be participatory and visible rather than voyeurist
and verbose. What "occidental theater," wrote Artaud in *The
Theater and Its Double*, "permits to be called language (with
that particular intellectual dignity generally ascribed to this
word) [is] only articulated language, grammatically articulated
language, i.e., the language of speech, speech which, pronounced or unpronounced, has no greater value than if it is
merely written."[31]

On dream interpretation, Freud wrote, "It is very note-
worthy how little the dream-work keeps to word-presentations;
it is always ready to exchange one word for another till it finds
the expression which is most handy for plastic representation";
and "The dream-content . . . is expressed as it were in a pictographic script."[32] Freud also pointed out that words were not
essential but almost incidental additions within the framework
of the dream; it is as if they belonged to a different sphere. "If

we reflect that the means of representation in dreams are principally visual images and not words, we shall see that it is even more appropriate to compare dreams with a system of writing than with a language. In fact the interpretation of dreams is completely analogous to the decipherment of an ancient pictographic script such as Egyptian hieroglyphs."[33] Both the Freud and Artaud passages come from Derrida's related essays in *Writing and Difference.* Countering the "metaphysics-of-presence" notion that spoken language comes first, Derrida shows that Artaud's theater of cruelty, like the dreams examined by Freud, is not primarily spoken but seen; writing, whether on this ideal stage or in the dreaming mind, is gesturelike, a matter of ritual, cabalistic rather than being merely the secondary representation of a once-present voice. Words in dreams are regarded as materials, things, stitched on and sticking out like bits of thread. This manner of perceiving words, to the letter, in bits and pieces, figuratively or literally, which comes out to be the same thing, *might as well* be called reptilian. The reptile *sees*, mythologically its sense of sight is always vision, never sense in the sense of logic. The reptile remains at the heart of mentation: although it can be repressed, it cannot be eliminated. The reptile is the heart of the evolutionary stripper, where body becomes mind. In daylight hours we forget our past, suppress our strange history with its frozen center of "reptilian" timelessness. But at night, living as dream lovers, what we are comes back to haunt or charm. The twisted logic of lizards, the sense of serpents lingers on.

Robomates

In another twist of evolutionary fate the mammal-coated reptilian brain may be married to ultramodern technology. Combining lifelike flesh based on advances in polymer chemistry with the artificial intelligence of sexual surrogates "who" may someday be produced to answer the baser needs of lonely human beings is a frightening—but real—possibility.

According to one future-oriented male chauvinist who was excited to share his thoughts on talk radio, "robomates" would be capable not only of cooking, cleaning, and tirelessly maintaining the house while their spouses sleep but would be able to simulate a mature emotionally fulfilling adult relationship— if it is possible to imagine, as this person does, having a mature relationship with a lifelike doll whose head may be replaced to satisfy a lust for sexual variety! According to the self-proclaimed "futurist," since Shintoism and Buddhism consider man's productions to be part of his soul, mass production of such ersatz humans is most likely to begin in Asian countries, such as Korea, which have an excellent capitalist industrial base in addition to their hospitable belief systems. The robomates would be the material enactment of the ancient Upanishad vision of God dividing into the man and woman in order to alleviate the boredom and loneliness of eternal Being.

We may speculate about human sexuality even though its opaque future is behind our backs as something we sense but cannot see. The ancient knot between reproduction and sexuality is preserved as humans evolve on one broad path. It is easy to imagine lovers languidly making love in zero-gravity space stations, doing it in positions impossible on Earth; it is easy to imagine also, the easier, reduced-gravity birth in space of infants conceived extraterrestrially, infants whose brains could perhaps develop differently under the different conditions of space. In another broad path, the knot may be cut, releasing the sexual impulse. Since future nation-states may attempt to control reproduction to preserve their power, sexuality, too, because of its ancient tie to reproduction, may be regulated; examples of this "first path" already exist, for instance in countries where birth control or sterilization is mandated. Such nation-state controls on our individual reproductive freedoms would be a repetition at a higher level of the "totalitarian biology" of animal bodies in which totipotency—the equal potential of all cells in a body to reproduce—is sacrificed to the reproduction of the whole. That humans may be cells in the body politics of nation-states is clearly a frightening possibility in terms of escalating infringements upon individual freedoms; think of conscription, mandatory drafting of nationally expendable young men in war, and, in general, of the "rights" exercised by countries (or gangs) upon the individuals that comprise them.

In A. E. Van Vogt's futuristic fantasy "The Human Operators," earthlings have forgotten their origins. Out of touch with their history, warm flesh-and-blood people tend the mechanical maintenance—essentially janitorial functions—of cybernetically self-conscious space vehicles. Nonetheless, the ancient knot between mammalian sexuality and reproduction remains intact. In this version of a sexual future, the reproduction of machines requires retention of human sexual reproduction—just as human reproduction retains the meiotic sexuality of two-billion-year-old microorganisms.

Either of these two broad paths—or both—may chart the human sexual future: in one reproduction and sexuality remain inextricable, and in the other reproduction and sexuality become progressively disentangled, unknotting until the one ultimately has little to do with the other. Unexpectedly, even more dramatic scenarios may occur. Only dimly can the possibilities of the human sexual future be envisaged. The reconstructed past is more illuminating and accessible. Ready now to reveal a still-deeper level of life behind the mask of animality, we strip the dancer of the seductive garment of reptilian and mammalian sexuality. Delving more deeply into our vertebrate heritage, we take a psychoanalytic detour to do double service in the next chapter. We (1) trace the evolutionary origins of the penis in amphibians and fish ancestral to reptiles and (2) examine the phallus as a vanishing point or blind spot in human minds.

5

PHALLIC
PSYCHE

Like the Tower of Babel, they knew what they were after.
—PATTI SMITH

Sexuality is the vanishing point of meaning.
—JACQUELINE ROSE

The evolutionary stripper turns to reveal an erect penis. "She" becomes a "he." The phallus, conspicuous in many ancestral bodies, is now gone. In its place float two fish holograms, swimming dreamily through the air. The fish are preceded by shimmering green amphibians and mercurial pools of water, reflecting the spot of light that hovers above the stage.

The evolutionary dancer has holographically undressed men and women to display the spectacle of our mammalian and reptilian innards. But in the darkened theater of motley flesh and Navajo time we have never been sure which figures portray our real prehistory and which remain mere vivid fantasies. Moreover, as we move beyond a hundred million years ago into the realm of reptiles, it becomes increasingly unclear what part of the dancing hologram is meant to represent body and what part mind. Now, as if to emphasize this confusion, the evolutionary

stripper devolves into an amphibious morass in the shape of a
lithe woman, then shatters and reforms into a gelatinous mass
of eggs, glittering like a million pearls. Dissolving, melding
together, the glittering caviar of amphibians becomes a smooth
silvery mirror. The spectators search the shining, laser-made
crystal for the clue to some secret meaning, but they find nothing
but the spectacle of their own inquisitive faces. The mirror melts
into streams of mercury that collect into a pool on the floor of
the stage. As the pool of quicksilver shrinks, two fish with mod-
ified limbs float over the stage, then land on it, catching the
air audibly as they prance rhythmically, in stylized fashion,
trying to see beyond the edge of the spotlight's comically moving
beam.

Psychoanalysis

The phallic psyche: in this chapter we will gingerly
take a step off the relatively solid ground of science into the
more speculative domain of psychoanalysis. Here we will become acquainted with some of the basic ideas of contemporary
psychoanalysis. In this chapter we learn not only of the evolution of the physical penis but of the phallus as a source of
symbols and meaning in the "timeless" unconscious. Since
the phallus is the most obvious organ of sexual reproduction,
it becomes a basis for childhood fantasies, and a focus for the
magical thinking studied by psychoanalysis. We will briefly
look at this magical thinking—the thinking that reveals itself
in jokes and dreams and Freudian "slips"—and see how it
seems to work by magic words and illusory mirrors. Then we
return to the more empirical description of the prehistory of
sexuality.

Is psychoanalysis just literature and poetry couched in the
presentable form of serious scientific discourse? No, not "just."
Psychoanalysis, as widely understood in Great Britain and the
United States, is a form of therapeutic expertise; but it is not
only a means of healing the sick. Psychoanalysis is alive and

well, now thriving in adulterated forms under names such as "deconstruction" and "literary criticism." The resurgence of the works of Freud, mainly due to French intellectuals, is not necessarily welcomed or even well known to English and American readers. Attitudes toward psychoanalysis are well illustrated by an anecdote told by the Canadian psychoanalyst Francois Peraldi. Peraldi describes a transatlantic encounter, a meeting of the minds between several French and several American psychoanalysts. Papers written by the participants had been distributed before the meeting, but a deep hush fell over the group when asked to begin. Finally, after several moments of silence, an American psychoanalyst spoke: "Well," he said, "we have read all your papers but we are sorry to say it is not psychoanalysis. It is literature." "We, too, have read your papers," replied a French psychoanalyst, "and it also is not psychoanalysis. It is medicine." Although psychoanalysis is differently interpreted, we believe that in it the spirit of scientific inquiry remains absolutely firm. Biology is a main pillar in the edifice of psychoanalytic thinking begun by Freud. But psychoanalysis goes beyond biology. Describing it Freud said psychoanalysis goes on and on; never coming to closure, stopping without ending, it demands patience and fortitude from those who would really undergo it.

Psychoanalysis occurs not only between analyst and analysand within the privacy and comfort of the analyst's office. Confirmation of an expensive and exclusive appointment in advance, the supine patient who "free-associates" from the reclining comfort of the couch, the private office of the stone-faced analyst jotting notes—these are, in a sense, mere embellishments, stereotypes of psychoanalysis, Freudian clichés. Authentic psychoanalysis—the exploratory breakdown of the "soul" or *psyche*—can also take place between authors and readers; one of the ways it does so is by a stream of consciousness—a presence of mind—followed by the abdication of authority. With the breakdown of the psyche, of authoritative answers, it becomes unclear who is speaking to whom. A book, too, is a psychoanalytical tool; it generates communication by provoking thought of oneself with oneself. Indeed, the words on a page of a book do not respond—they are irresponsible—like the attentive but taciturn psychoanalyst. The payment of money, Freud insisted, alters the nature of personal and emotional ties, underscoring the professional detachment of the analyst. And yet expenditure is important not only to the success of psychoanalysis but to the acquisition of a book such as this: so p(l)ay attention. Psychoanalysis was dubbed by one of its first patients as "the talking cure." Might it not also be, in keeping with these parallels, a "writing cure"?

The Phallus in Magical Thinking

For psychoanalysis the phallus, the penis as symbol, is "the missing something"—that ever-elusive satisfier that permanently sustains desire precisely because it is never really obtained. Examining its evolutionary origin, we see how, in the ancestors to reptiles, the penis appeared in evolutionary time. Piercing the superficial genitals and indeed the entirety of the body we will continue to search for a missing something in the microbial layers that form the "heart" of sex as it is physiologically or biologically construed. And yet psychoanalysis warns us that such a search may be interminable, revealing no final key or golden treasure at the end of the researcher's quest. To understand the absence of finality, we make a detour along the none-to-pithy path of psychoanalysis.

Evolutionary biolgists, we have learned, insist that the penis because of its crucial role in reproduction is of greater importance to survival than is the clitoris. But does this high survival value afforded the penis support Freud's view of "the" unconscious mind? Psychoanalysis, like evolutionary biology, emphasizes the primary importance of childhood views of the penis—or rather, the phallus, the penis as symbol. Phallic symbols for Freud are virtually omnipresent, especially in their absence. Indeed, the young girl's view of male genitalia leads her to presume that she is inadequate, castrated, missing something of vital importance. For Freud this castration takes on special significance. Freud called the female's desire to replace the lost phallus *"penisneid."* Translated, this is "penis envy," but that appellation is too literal. The phallic symbol is not simply an object that can transpose or transmute into any number of cylindrical forms. When Freud was asked if his cigar were a phallic symbol he commented, "Sometimes a cigar is just a cigar."

For Jacques Lacan desire is always desire of the other and this means, often enough, desire of the mother, the first love object; since the mother lacks the phallus, the child, whatever its sex, wants initially nothing less than to *be* the phallus for the mother. The child realizes that he or she comes out of the place where the father with his penis goes in. The reason the child wants to be the phallus is simple. He or she thus magically associates him- or herself with the male organ. Having the phallus, as boys do, is already a form of castration, since it does not satisfy the desire of the mother. Thinking magically, children identify themselves with what goes in or comes out of the mother's body. At the same time they realize the inadequacy of this identification. Psychoanalysis is largely an attempt to explore the magical thinking of the child that lingers on in the adult.

The male corollary to *penisneid* is the "castration complex": the little boy revels in his penis, he adores it but feels its inadequacy and fears he will lose it, as (he believes) his mother did. Desiring to be one with the mother, the threat of penis loss is his just punishment for wishing his father away. But since the boy's penis only approximates and is not the real organ desired by the mother, Lacan argues, not only girls but "everyone is castrated."[1] Psychological health requires accepting the reality of these magical thoughts of castration, not in the sense of acknowledging the absence of genitals but in the sense of being aware of a permanent inadequacy in the realm of desire—especially on the level of language. Acceptance of "castration" means coming to grips with the repressed childhood thoughts of permanent inadequacy and loss.

The psychoanalytic phallus thus need not be a penis. Since it means or points to something other than itself, it is not self-identical. In the unconscious mind, as explicated by psycho-analysis, the phallus is always on the verge of something else. The "surreal" dream logic of the phallus can be appreciated by looking at René Magritte's 1942 painting *La Mer* (The ocean) of a reclining nude male whose penis is a woman. Freud claimed that the shoe of a shoe-fetishist signifies the "woman's (mother's) phallus in which the little boy once believed and does not wish to forego."[2] Beyond Freud, Lacan wrote, "We know that the unconscious castration complex has the function of a knot." Mischievously, the word Lacan uses for "knot," *noeud,* is a well-known French slang term for penis.[3] Both Freud and Lacan use their writings not just to describe but actually to enact a kind of psychoanalysis with their readers. By contrast, most psychoanalytic publications in England and America engage in a dry scientific style in which each word or sign is naively assumed to have only a single—and controllable—meaning. But psychoanalysis cannot engage in an objective understanding of the child's magical understanding. It catches the contagion of the unconscious, surreal, illogical thoughts it studies. One often feels in reading apologists for psychoanalysis that they protest too much when they proclaim its scientific status. And yet chemistry has its roots in the unreasonable formulas and ceaseless experimentation of alchemists; astronomy deceives itself if it thinks itself free of the ancient astrological need to find cosmic and mathematical correspondences between the universe and the individual.[4] No science—and especially no writing of science—is immune from magical thinking.

Mirrorings

The phallus is the signifier "which has no signified." In his essay "The Meaning of the Phallus," Lacan emphasizes Freud's discovery of an irreducible "disturbance of human sexuality." This disturbance is "insoluble by any reduction to biological givens."[5] Yet Lacan explains desire—of which the missing phallus is, from one point of view, the cause—by resorting to biological parable. Seeing itself in reflection as a unified whole, a complete body, the infant, according to Lacan, is overcome by jubilant feelings of mastery, independence, and self-control. The whole reflection contrasts sharply with the fragmentation, uncoordination, and psychic dismemberment of all the infant's previous perceptions. For Lacan, however, the crucial feature of this jubilation is its lack of foundation, its basis in illusion: the infant's perceived unity is out of step with its reality as a dependent, fractured being living in a world of perceptual non sequiturs. The baby sees itself where it is *not*: upon the reflective plane of a mirror. The child's ecstasy in the face of the mirror is the founding trick of the glorious but ultimately illusory experience of selfhood. For Lacan, the self is "decentered," it is not where it appears to be. The image of wholeness is just that: an image.

Lacan's "mirror stage" need not refer to a real glass mirror. The sense of identity and control is achieved in other ways: identification with a well-coordinated mother or other identifiably whole body. Feelings of mastery, of control, may resurge frequently in adult life, but they are always supported by the founding self-delusions of the mirror stage. Mastery, for Lacan, is always image-inary—not just "imaginary" but a special term he uses in contrast with "symbolic" and "real." It is a product of the association and identification of the mirror stage. The real I is not there or changing; it is a black letter or word, the literary equivalent of a hologram.

The mirror stage posited by Lacan relies on that peculiarity of human development discussed earlier under the name of "neoteny." Neotenous humans, remember, are those who, as adults, retained juvenile characteristics of their ape ancestors such as broad forehead, small jaws, canine teeth, and naked skin. "Actually," writes Nobel laureate François Jacob, "some of the most dramatic events in evolution resulted from a change by which sexual maturity was achieved at an earlier developmental stage, so that previously embryonic characteristics were retarded in the adult, while previously adult characteristics were lost."[6] The mirror stage is based on this "real *specific prematurity of birth* in man."[7] Many mammals walk, even run, within minutes or hours of their births, but humans, although the sense of vision quickly develops, remain helpless and hopelessly uncoordinated for more than a year. No two-year-old alone survives. The five-year-old can never feed or warm herself. Human infants are born too soon—at a stage of development when ape-relatives are safely tucked away in utero. Left alone, unable to move about or fend for itself, the human infant is nonetheless immersed in a startling display of visual imagery beyond control—a kind of psychedelic light show for a disembodied consciousness. In the mirror stage the confused infant, at the mercy of another whose breast and gaze have not yet been differentiated from itself, perceives itself in the "mirror" of the maternal body with a gleeful sense of individuality. But this glee is based on false impressions.

Moreover, the child not only receives this ecstatic, image-inary sense of being "me" from the encounter with the mirror. The encounter with the mirror also places him or her in a time frame. The baby's frightening view of itself as being in "bits and pieces"—as in either a nightmare or a painting by Hieronymous Bosch—only occurs in retrospect, *after* the joyful encounter with an imaginary wholeness. As the American literary critic Jane Gallop writes, "What appears to precede the mirror stage is simply a projection or reflection. There is nothing on the other side of the mirror."[8] "What matters," Lacan writes, "when one tries to elaborate upon some experience, isn't so much what one understands, as what one doesn't understand."[9]

If Lacanian notions such as the mirror stage or the phallic signifier are found disturbing, remember that Lacan's writings are a sort of a rebus, a picture-puzzle, and that the effort to make sense of them, to discover or invent a subtext, is *more* important than the superficial content. They are, in the parlance of literary criticism, "semiotically open texts." From this point of view the mirror stage is a metaphor of ignorance; it is as if Lacan were saying to us, "Look, I'll show you how this trick of the self, of identity is done: with mirrors." But when we go to look at the mirror Lacan provides for an explanation, we are still not quite sure if Lacan is putting us on or off—if the production of the mirror is itself a trick.

Symbols

The mirror stage is recognized by the violent disruption in the succeeding symbolic stage. The smooth "image-inary" relation between the ego and its images and between mother and child are ruptured abruptly by the fracturing and fragmenting of the father with his phallus and symbols. While similitude and identification is in the mirror stage, these break in the symbolic realm where fragmented speech and the realization of incompleteness replace the illusory wholeness of a mirror. Just as the little boy's penis is only a phallic signifier and not the father's penis, so the symbols and language of the symbolic realm are not the desired things themselves but only their signs.

The important identification of the psychoanalyst with the father, or the mother, or some other "significant other"—an identification that in traditional Freudian psychoanalysis is called "transference"—is part of the Lacanian image-inary. The ego—your "I"—identifies with imagoes, idealized mental images. But these images also break: the analyst is not your father, your child is not you or your younger brother. Entering Lacan's symbolic realm we recognize the artificiality and overlap of our deepest personal identifications, and we perhaps treat others with greater awareness.

Lacan's category of the symbolic resembles the Freudian Oedipal complex after which it is modeled. Though disruptive and fragmenting, the symbolic successor to the image stage is a necessary rite of psychological passage. Symbolization for Lacan resembles weaning; just as in the absence of the mother the rubber nipple comforts the anxious infant, the spoken words of the father provide a mixed relief. The infant begins to recognize the trick of language. Words supplement and supplant, they simultaneously designate and replace the missing objects they represent. Learning to symbolize, children cut their ties, and reconciling themselves to a chronic lack of maternal satisfaction, realize that there is no end to desire. They may identify with the speaking father—a switch by which they appropriate what once threatened them.

As words substitute for things, so the father's spoken and written law substitutes for the mother. This law is singularly prohibitive; *"le nom du père"* in Lacanian lingo literally means "the name of the father," but in spoken French the phrase sounds indistinguishable from "the 'no' of the father." The father figure by his very presence intrudes and says no to the child. And the part that stands for the whole in this troubling intrusion is the phallus, the *noeud*, the knot. For Lacan, the phallus begins the entire process of signification. A symbolic sword, severing continuous contact with the mother, it penalizes. But this phallic sword cuts both ways; by employing phallic, paternal symbolization it appropriates paternal power and the Oedipal complex is alleviated, if not resolved.

Lacan accused American psychoanalysis of betraying Freud's insights. According to Lacan, they distorted Freudian theory by deemphasizing the importance of the unconscious and of infant sexuality. American "ego analysts," by treating the Oedipus complex as a childhood phase to be outgrown in the move to a mature and healthy ego, deny the phallic signification as a continuous psychic reality. But language itself is phallic. It interrupts the primal union of the mother and child. Language, by continuously replacing and displacing what is longed for—by endlessly substituting signs—works through metaphor and metonymy. Between the lines, in the subtext—on these sheets, between these covers—is the yearning for possession of that which cannot quite be grasped. Like the Hebrew prohibition against displaying the name of God, to write anything already obviates almost all of the rest, is a betrayal, a careless slip of the writing hand. Lacan spoke of Freud's Copernican revolution as being greater than Darwin's: consciousness is eccentric, it has no center. *Ça parle: it* (the unconscious) *speaks*. At the center of human being, there is a w(hole). Disfiguring language—poeticized, perversely punctuated, incomplete, or overflowing—helps reconcile us to our unavoidable "castration." This is because such language studiously avoids the mirage of wholeness. As they say in show business, it leaves us wanting more . . .

Phallic Variety

The phallus, as we have seen, is crucial to the early magical perception of the psyche. But what of its biological cognate, the penis? How did it evolve? Both the penis and its relatively large size in humans may be the result of sperm competition. First, let's look at the human penis. In sexually very active early human societies, men with large erections (but not larger than the vaginal passage) would have gained a slight advantage in impregnating women. Inheriting their genes, the male children of these women would have been likely to grow into men with penises closer to the size of their fathers than those of ancestral apemen.

While sperm competition may adequately explain the greater relative size of human penises, evolutionists had earlier made some other suggestions: (1) that women, viewing naked males, selected as lovers those with the largest penises, (2) that males with large penises displayed them, frightening smaller-penised rivals, and (3) that females chose large-membered males because, facing frontward, these large-penised males could bring them to sexual climax. All these hypotheses are relatively unsatisfactory. Since most women, at least when queried in a woman's magazine survey, claimed to be less attracted to penis size than to other male anatomical features, the "attraction hypothesis" is easy to dismiss. The survey requiring women to rate male attributes they found sexiest reported only a 2 percent preference for penises, compared to a 39 percent interest in buttocks; the women were more attracted to broad shoulders and buttock shape than large penis size. Although comparative data on human penis size from race to race are limited, female choice of men with large penises is apt to be most conspicuous in tropical climates. This is because women in the tropics are more apt to see males nude and judge their penises.

The "scare" hypothesis also seems unlikely: muscular men with small penises seldom cower in the presence of skinny weaklings with large ones. Unlike some other primates, human males are not known to threaten each other with erections.

Even less tempting is the hypothesis that large penises enhanced female pleasure during sexual intercourse. Penis dimension is neither the major determinant of female sexual pleasure, nor is a big penis a guarantee of female pleasure. As Stephen Jay Gould emphatically points out, the existence of an anatomical trait does not *necessarily* mean that it was an adaptation—that it conferred any benefits upon the survival of those possessing it. The sperm competition explanation for penis size is the most elegant. The vagina is, believe it or not, a very hostile place for sperm; it is acidic, a veritable obstacle course or torture chamber so full of pitfalls that most of the time not a single of the hundreds of millions of sperm ejaculated survive. A penis that reaches the back walls of the vagina therefore has an advantage over one that ejaculates its contents further from the egg. The advantage of delivering copious quantities of sperm close to the egg creates the evolutionary conditions for growth in penile length—although a penis that reaches beyond the back walls of the vagina offers no additional advantage. Human penises, unlike those of some other primates, are displayed outside the body cavity, and are therefore unusually vulnerable to injury. Our male ancestors may have had penis bones, as many mammals today do, but lost them and the fold of skin covering them in the abdominal area.

Two out of three men estimate their penis to be undersized, according to physician Barry McCarthy, author of a book on male sexual awareness.[10] McCarthy attributes penis-size anxiety to several factors. First, boys catch sight of their fathers' penises at an impressionable age and worry they won't "catch up." Second, glances at other males in locker rooms are made end-on: the other men's penises seem larger because a man sees his own from above, a perspective that makes the penis seem smaller because of the shift known to artists as fore-shortening. Third, flaccid penises vary dramatically in size; erect, there is far less variation: the average human erect penis measures thirteen centimeters (five to six inches). Fourth, men are kept in ignorance by a general male reluctance to openly discuss intimate sexual matters with each other: men are more likely to tell women about penis preoccupation than they are to tell other men; and so the myth persists that large penis size enhances female pleasure.

There is much phallic variety in the biological world. Many different kinds of "penises" exist: the aedeagus of flies, mites, and butterflies, the cloacal protuberances of some frogs, the copulatory organ of the domestic honey bee drone (which suicidally breaks off and blocks all others from mating the queen), the embolus of the golden web spider, the anal fins (gonopodia) of fishes, the double hemipenes of snakes, the intromittent organs of fish and rodents, the ligula of the drag-onfly. All are penises or phallic organs, used to transmit male sperm to females. Phallic variety extends from tiny protuber-ances to whale penises, which, though usually kept tucked away inside the body, can reach six feet in length. Ostrich males are also well endowed, so much so, in fact, that walking sticks have been fashioned from their genitalia.

The genitalia of insects are more diverse than those of mam-mals. The females of many insect species have "sperm storage organs," special sites that incubate sperm, keeping it alive for months prior to fertilization. Because of the remoteness of these female organs, male insects have evolved special fluted and scooplike members that bear little resemblance in form to a mammalian penis. Many times in vastly different animals unique scooping and pumping penises capable of displacing previously deposited sperm have evolved. For example, in the Zygoptera, predaceous insects in the order Odonata comprising damselflies and dragonflies, the penis has a scooplike section at the end that acts to pull clumps of competing sperm from one or both of the female's sperm storage organs. Similarly the penis bone of many mammals—the baculum—may act as a cleaning mechanism to rid the female of competing sperm.

The members of certain species of rodents and of butterflies are so ornately different in their juxtaposition of spines, curves, and fluting that as an important taxonomic tool they serve to distinguish between otherwise very similar-looking animals. The best taxonomic indicator for some species is penis shape, which evolved as males competed for access to female eggs. And there is so much variation in the size, shape, and function of damselfly penises that a qualified entomologist can identify species solely on the basis of the male organ.

The great variety of insect organs results from the mechanics of their copulation, combined with sexual selection. If it is the right size and shape, the penoid organ of another male can dislodge previously stored sperm from the sperm storage sites of insect females.

The Swedish seed bug *(Lygaeus equestris)* avoids coitus interruptus: the male has a member that not only stretches to fully two-thirds the length of his body (equivalent to a four-foot-long penis in a man!), but is replete with hooks that prevent him from being dislodged once he has engaged the female. Partner seed bugs remain joined by the male's well-placed penis for up to twenty-four hours.

Such rococo traits and macho ruses seem to have evolved as means of gaining control over sometimes reluctant female bodies; although animal sex may entail the sacrificial death of the male during the copulation, the steep price is evolutionarily worth it if it is the only way to get potentially immortal genes into the next generation. Spiky ornamentation has even developed in sperm. Snail's sperm comes adorned with backward-pointing spines that presumably act as a barbed arrowpoint to anchor one male's cells inside his female despite subsequent matings by other males.

In evolution, as in military technology, behaviors and biotechnologies occasionally appear that quickly make obsolete the highly elaborate tactics of the past. The repeater rifle, the Gatling gun, and barbed wire rendered cavalry obsolete, just as the stirruped cavalry in its turn had outmoded foot soldiery. Comparable innovations mark the twists and turns of reproductive fate in the ancient "flowery combat" of the sexes.

Consider the sexual weaponry that has evolved in the fluke *Moniliformis dubius*, a parasitic flatworm that lives in vertebrate digestive systems. These flukes plug not only the genital tracts of their females, but those of other males—as if in medieval times, chastity belt makers, enamored of their clever handiwork, had developed a model suitable for both sexes!

A most bizarre example of insect sexual weirdness is *Xylocoris maculipennis*, the African bedbug. Males possess spearlike organs with which they stab and penetrate the abdomens of females. This drastic procedure creates de facto "vaginas"— in fact, puncture wounds—at various places in female bodies. The sperm enter through such a puncture wound, swimming through the female's hemolymph, the bloodlike body fluid. Traveling about, some reach her sperm-storage organ. There they are duly stored. The genes of the stabbers are propagated by male offspring that also possess daggerlike penises.

Such behavior must have killed ancestral female bedbugs. Yet today African bedbug females have evolved a special pad of female abdominal tissue (the "organ of Berlese") that helps them heal. Female bedbugs possibly even use protein in the ejaculate as nutrition to help nourish their eggs. These blood-sucking denizens of third-rate hotels have also changed the rules of the mating game in another way. Using those same spearlike genitals, male African bedbugs routinely puncture other males, forcefully ejecting their sperm into the victim's abdomen. Male–male forced matings are of course sterile; at first glance such sex seems to be gratuitous in the Darwinian game of leaving the most offspring. But bedbug sperm, unlike that of mammals, may survive for years inside the victim's hemolymph. Merging with the victim's sperm, the rapist's sperm is ejaculated by proxy, through another male's penis. And so it is that the bedbug genes, promoting what in human terms would be homosexual rape, are perpetuated into the next bedbug generation.

Most of the variation in phallic shape and function is found in insects; it is less striking in mammals. In vertebrates generally the contents of the ejaculate disperse throughout the female's reproductive system but sperm is not stored.

Evolving Penises
and Cementing Semen

Human penises did not evolve from bedbug "syringes" or other insect protrusions. The reproductive organs of men came from those of fish and later amphibian ancestors. The first penises, of which those of humans are an evolutionary elaboration, were naturally selected as they increasingly ensured fertilization of eggs. Before penises evolved, sperm was disseminated relatively randomly in water, by the fish and amphibians that were ancestral to reptiles and mammals. External fertilization—release of sperm into egg-filled water— preceded the internal fertilization in which males, equipped with penises, ejaculate sperm directly into the female body. "The penis itself might have evolved in response to sperm competition, males able to insert sperm further into the female tract and therefore closer to the ova being favored," writes Geoff A. Parker, the innovator of sperm competition theory.[11]

Receding into prehistory the phallus seems to disappear into the body of the evolutionary stripper. The human line extends beyond australopithecine apes to tree-dwelling primates and the first night-stalking small mammals, who themselves had evolved from the same stem reptiles that later gave rise to the dinosaurs. Beyond prosimian primates our human lineage is traced to tree-dwelling shrewlike mammals not too unlike rodents. Interestingly, males of some modern rodent species leave special mating "plugs"—gluey, sticky secretions that would bar access of other rodent males to already-inseminated females were it not that these same male rodents have also evolved special penile spines whose sole function seems to be the removal of the mating plugs. Is the peculiar stickiness of human semen, which becomes gluelike soon after ejaculation, which can mat and dry to skin and hair, a result of its ability to block future ejaculates? Drone bees leave behind both their genitalia and a sealing mucuslike substance as they mate with the queen immediately prior to their death. Compare such mortal plugging up in bees to the obsessive guarding of females by frogs of the genus *Atelopus*; even after eggs are amply fertilized by sperm, these frogs will not let go; they continue for months to clamp on to their mates. Perhaps the viscous consistency of human semen likewise derives from our remote mammal ancestors whose semen "cemented," functioning as a kind of natural chastity belt, barring or limiting access to would-be future impregnators.

Since the first penislike organs probably appeared in amphibians transitional between water-dwelling fish and land-inhabiting reptiles, the mating patterns of existing amphibians may provide clues to penis origins. In most frogs and toads, called anurans, fertilization is external to the body; the male grasps the female from the back in a kind of long-lasting hug, called amplexus. He stays there until the female spawns, at which time he sheds sperm into the water and onto the eggs. During amplexus he may be harassed by other males attempting to push him off. This behavior of frogs and toads varies from that of the two other living orders of amphibians, the apodans and the urodeles. In both these later orders, fertilization is internal: it occurs within the body of the female. Male urodeles, including the salamanders and newts, fertilize the eggs inside the bodies of their females, but without a penis. Males instead transfer a spermatophore, a special pouch that contains bitter sperm in a sweet package of nutriment. Urodele males excrete the packages, usually leaving them as "gifts" on moist ground for the females to pick them up, eat them, and incorporate them into their bodies. (Strange as this behavior sounds to us, it has independently evolved, in almost precisely the same form, in many species of insects.) Salamander and newt amphibians display a wide variety of reproductive behaviors; the urodele group includes both water- and land-mating species. In the legless amphibians, the apodans, sperm is transferred directly into the female cloaca by means of a penislike "intromittent organ."

The fertilization that occurs in mammals inside the female body evolved from external fertilization. In the external fer-

tilization of fish such as the bluegill sunfish, the fourspine
stickleback, and the blenny, eggs are released in the open water
away from the body of the female; sperm fertilizes them in the
open. When such fish spawn, small opportunistic males often
rush into the vicinity shedding their own sperm on the eggs.
Some marine animals, for example, cartilaginous fish such as
sharks and rays (Chondricythes), have penislike organs, yet
most male fish still release milt into the water where external
fertilization occurs. With the evolution of amphibians from
fish, ejaculation inside female bodies became more prevalent
as males competed to get nearer and nearer to eggs. Males
supplanted each other. As eggs were reached even before their
release into the water, those males whose sperm reached them
tended to leave more offspring. Sperm-placing intromittent
organs long enough to preempt other males offered a reproductive advantage. The amphibians ancestral to reptiles and
mammals most likely had such penis-precursor intromittent
organs.

Another factor in the natural selection of internal fertilization and penislike organs in some species of ancestral amphibians was the harshness of the open air. Early forms of
land-crawling fish and amphibians died, their sperm and eggs
destroyed by solar radiation, desiccated or dispersed by winds.
In organisms that returned to water for mating, fertilization
and early development of the embryos fared better. Penises in
other lineages may have first appeared in fish-headed amphibious ancestors, forced to survive on land as their natural
aquatic habitats dried out. Although the adults live on tree
bark, around the edges of ponds, on lily pads, or in the leaf
litter of the forest floor, the vast majority of amphibians return
to the water to breed.

Ocean cruisers, sandy beaches, and waterfalls still attract
lovers. Perhaps water remains seductive because of its ancient
link to animal reproduction. Males ejaculate a whitish fluid
harboring haploid sperm cells that recall the four-fifths of Earth
history during which life was solely microbial: moist, unpro-
tected by hard shells or skin, protist life in the Proterozoic eon
was vulnerable to the crackling heat and winds of dry land.

Many fully terrestrial animals, such as land turtles, salamanders, and tree frogs, return to water to lay their eggs. In our lineage, the fetus floats in an amniotic universe so warm and serene it is the very symbol of security and well-being. In this aquatic paradise, the fertilized egg develops, recalling the form and lifestyle of its amphibian ancestors, even to the point of resembling a tadpole. Like childbirth, human sexuality, which literally brings out the wetness of our bodies' insides, has been described as an "oceanic" experience.

Sperm-placement also arose in aquatic habitats in the absence of the penis. Male octopuses, not mammals at all but mollusks, use their tentacles to insert sperm into the orifices of female octopuses. Male octopi engaging in this act turn bright red. The example of the octopus shows that land dwelling is not a prerequisite for the evolution of fertilization within the body. Internal fertilization is more efficient, less wasteful, and, when it does evolve, tends to relegate males that do not practice it to the trash bin of male sexual evolution. The ancestors of sea horses and other teleost fish also independently evolved internal fertilization.

Once penises appeared, in many lineages they evolved to become highly ornate. Some penises may shoot sperm by propulsive ejaculation considerably further than their own length. Some lizard penises are bright blue. The sexual organs of some insects are longer than the rest of their bodies. The dogfish sprays a "spermicidal douche" that reduces a previous male's ability to deposit, displace, or dilute sperm. Penises and other sperm-placing organs vary more in shape and size than virtually any other part of animal anatomy.

Not only have male organs evolved. Female reproduction organs display a dazzling variety of patterns, too. The age-old struggle of males to oust each other to enter first is not always to the females' liking. By secluding the site in which fertilization takes place, and by evolving intricate flanges, flaps, and sphincters, the female genitals of some species are veritable obstacle courses for sperm. Both male and female reproductive systems have, of course, evolved; but since, in people, most of the female reproductive system is internal, whereas the male

reproductive system includes a penis and testicles conspicu-
ously exposed on the outside of the body, the male genitalia
play a greater role in the magical, associative thinking of the
child.

Strange Bedfellows

But since the phallus is a focus of the magical thinking of the child, the evolutionary biological search for penis
origins remains frustrating, if somewhat enchanted. The quest
for the origin of the penis remains unresolved, in part, because
fossil penis bones are not known in human ancestors, in part,
because the main, fleshy part of the penis is not likely to be
preserved anyway. Even in cultural artifacts, such as ancient
Roman or Florentine sculptures of nudes, the penis tends to
break off—often it was broken off by Christians—leaving the
imagination alone to provide it.

For Lacan, psychoanalysis was a demi-science, still exciting,
not yet rigidified but having to borrow its models from other
sciences such as archeology and linguistics because it was still
"in labor," a new science undergoing the sociocultural difficulties of its birth. In "The Topic of the Imaginary," Lacan
exhorts his colleagues: "My dear fellows, you wouldn't believe
what you owe to geology. If it weren't for geology, how could
one end up thinking that one could move, on the same level,
from a recent to a much more ancient layer? It wouldn't be
a bad thing, I note in passing, if every analyst went out and
bought a small book on geology. There was once an analyst
geologist, Leuba, who wrote one. I can't recommend you to
read it too highly." In another seminar, Lacan compared his
great mentor Sigmund Freud to a careful archeologist who
puts back in its proper place—unlike some followers—each
of the fascinating artifacts he digs up.[12] Yet after digging up
the field of evolutionary biology in quest of the origins of the
penis, we are left curiously unsatisfied. It is almost as if, after
extensive excavation, we have returned empty-handed. Having

found the penis of evolutionary biology, we lack the phallus of psychoanalysis. If the phallus is, as psychoanalysis purports, an object so obscure it is not even clear it is an object at all, then perhaps this feeling of loss—reminiscent of waking empty-handed from a dream of glittering coins—or image-ining a colorful holographic stripper from black-and-white text—is perfectly appropriate. Fundamentally different types of discourse, psychoanalysis and evolutionary biology resist merging: like the mind, which contains the body, which con-tains the mind, psychoanalysis and evolutionary biology each in turn attempt to engulf the other, but, like possessive lovers, neither ever fully succeeds.

Lingering Phallic Worship

Freud began his career studying the electrochem-istry of nerve cells, but such empirical studies did not sustain him. His office in Vienna was stacked with hundreds of objects: archeological remains, African carvings, figurines of wise men, statuettes of mythological characters, and ornamental pieces of glass. He compared his discovery of the unconscious and the secret language of dreams to the deciphering of Egyptian hieroglyphics of the Rosetta stone. It is easily imagined that Freud's collection had a *hermas*, a limbless Greek sculpture, a carved figure with a penis but missing arms and legs. Hermas were commonly found outside dwellings in ancient Greece. The square-shaped stone pillars were surmounted by a bust or head, especially of Hermes (Hermes—associated with the Egyptian scholar Hermes Trismegistos, as well as the philo-sophical practice of hermaneutics—was the messenger among the gods, presiding over roads, commerce, invention, elo-quence, and theft, and conducting the dead to Hades, the underworld.) The hermas or herms were part of a generalized cult in ancient Greece that included not only icons but phallic festivals and hymns of worship. In the spring of 415 B.C., however, vandals ravaged Athens and destroyed nearly all the hermas.

In ancient Scandinavia phallic worship was also present, as attested to by stone and bronze carvings. Ritual scenes depict men with axes, men with ploughs, men on ships; the men almost always bear both erections and swords.[13] Even the earliest great and anonymous artwork of human beings, the cave paintings of Lascaux, depicts a falling bird-headed man with erect phallus in the presence of a speared bison. Although proud, public, overt phallic worship has declined, covert phallicism is an inalienable, if unconscious, part of the Western European–American heritage, as Lacan and Freud insist.

Named for the American president, the Hoover Tower on the campus of Stanford University is often referred to as Hoover's last erection. Was there not something phallic in Kennedy's program to send Americans to the moon? Companies and venture capitalists vie with each other to build the highest skyscrapers—the tallest towers. Bombs, rockets, and guns, undeniably of more interest to boys and men than to girls and women, also bear an unmistakable resemblance to the erect ejaculating penis.

The Sun

What then is the meaning of the phallus? For Lacan the phallus was an "object" so central to the magical psyche that its meaning was plastic, unfixed, labile. The phallus is a "signifier without a signified." It is, in other words, a pure symbol that can mean anything and therefore finally nothing.

Male baboons at the periphery of a troop have been recorded frightening members from neighboring troops by spreading their legs to grip and point their erect penises. We have already seen that, mistaking himself for a stranger, a squirrel monkey, even a youngster who has never seen another male, will similarly display his erection to the mirror in greeting. In April of 1876 the naturalist J. von Fischer wrote in *Der Zoologische*

Garten that the first time a young male mandrill of his beheld himself in a looking glass, he turned around and presented his red rear end to the mirror. Darwin read of this "mooning" and wrote to Fischer, wondering what could be the meaning of such an "indecorous habit."[14] Fischer replied that he had other monkeys with equally embarrassing habits. He had taken pains, he wrote, to cure one *Macacus rhesus* of the inappropriate behavior, but the monkey continued to display its colorful rear end to strange persons and new monkeys. Fischer concluded that it must be some form of greeting. The meaning of the phallus remains as obscure as this monkey habit of displaying the backside. The phallus can be erotic arrow or indicator, a source for all pointing. Veiled in a condom, it functions transcendentally, in that its sense has been removed from procreation. The phallus can be pillar, erector, cigar, hose, tool, bone, feces, limb, person. Perhaps the most innovative use of the special qualities of phallic signification to date has been accomplished by Georges Bataille, an early member of the Surrealist movement who later diverged because he felt the Surrealists were too narrow. For Bataille the entire evolutionary odyssey of humanity from low-lying bacteria to *Homo erectus* represents an erection; this erection, however, is imperfect, since the eyes of human beings are still parallel to the ground and unable to stand the sight of their true aim, the blinding sun. The sun is the most abstract and erotic object we know, suggests Bataille, since we are drawn to it but cannot look at it, since we lift ourselves toward it but never reach it.

For Bataille the odyssey of humanity would be complete if the pineal gland in the forebrain opened up and the contents of the human body came ejaculating out toward the sun. This would be the logical conclusion of phallic human evolution. Bataille's connection of the sun with sexuality is not completely ludicrous. Indeed, the sexual excitement of "spring fever" can now be provisionally traced to physiology. Corresponding with the blossoms and perfumed air are the longer days of spring; and the sun, shining later in the day, has a specific effect on humans. Exposed to light, a portion of the brain called the superchiasmatic nucleus stimulates the pineal gland to reduce its production of melatonin, which acts as a sex entrainer or inhibitor. Arresting of melatonin production is especially sensitive to light late in the day, with the result that erotic intoxication may be a seasonally conditioned response to the brilliant sunlight and bright colors of spring. Nonetheless Bataille's idea of solar sexuality, his notion of the sun as the locus of human desire is clearly intended as a cosmic fable. A phallic fantasy.[15] Far less fantastic and phallic but equally striking are the stories of cellular pleasure to be told next, in which protists cannibalized each other and bacteria engaged in rampant, if desperate, sexual practices under the radiant influence of the blazing sun.

6

SUBVISIBLE SURVIVORS

'Tis the tempestuous loveliness of terror,
Far from the serpents gleams a brazen glare
Kindled by that inextricable error,
Which makes a thrilling vapour of the air.

—SHELLEY

In a yet deeper phase, the evolutionary stripper slides out of the snakeskin and fish scales—revealing a still more primordial level of sexuality, the ancient mutual gorging, writhing fusions, and tragicomic doubleness of single-celled beings. Beneath the cabalistic lizards squirm the cannibalistic protists. Devouring each other in a fertilization act, two attracted cells mate and their nuclei fuse. Tugging and moist inside, the fused cell secretes a single hardening wall that protects it from the viciousness of winter. And yet within these encapsulating fusing protists lies a still more primeval sexuality. The evolutionary stripper now discards a dazzling sunlit cover to show his still deeper level of sexuality: liquid patches of bargaining bacteria fluidly trading their genes. Finally, removing everything, the gender-flipping stripper stands stark naked.

According to linguists, the English word *love* has its origin in *luba,* the ancient Nostratic word for thirsty. Spoken some four-

teen thousand years ago, Nostratic is the proposed mother tongue for the Indo-European, Near East, and northern Asian language families. Although fourteen thousand years ago is but a moment for the evolutionary stripper, the correspondence between love and thirst is far older. Over a billion years before the origin of any languages, protists—microbes with nuclei— were engaging in cellular fusion in order to stave off thirst. Cellular fusion, as we see in this final routine of the evolutionary stripper, is the precursor and perhaps the model for all of later love. Desperately doubled protists, their nuclei erotically merged, stand at the core of our body and being. Dried out and thirsty, protists swallowed each other and some merged, becoming "diploid," as one.

Long before any protists, bacteria engaged in their peculiar form of sex as they were scorched by light from the hot sun. This chapter examines both these remote protists and their ancestors, the genetically recombining bacteria. Along the way, for the sake of completeness, we raise the old question of why sex even exists at all.

Sexual Alternatives

Renegade surrealists, mystical philosophers, and many scientists have pursued the meaning of sex. Baffled by the apparent wastefulness of finding a mate and competing with others to do so, biologists especially are tempted to devise explanations for sex. The eighteenth century naturalist Georges Buffon resisted this temptation. Regarding the question of sex, he wrote "that there is no other solution than the fact itself." But Buffon was exceptional.

As the Darwinian theory of evolution prevailed, biologists began to ask: "How did sex evolve?" and "Why, once it did evolve, was it retained in sexually reproducing populations?" Sex would not have come about "just to have the fun of banging two bacteria together. It's got to be fundamentally important at the genetic level—or God's playing a trick on us," remarked Norton Zinder, a molecular geneticist at Rockefeller University. The bizarre sex lives of microbes—bacteria, protists, fungi—show great variation on the theme of sexuality and gender; more than two sexes in many is the rule. *Schizophyllum*, a transsexual fungal growth of dying trees and fallen logs, for example, has over seventy thousand sexes; some common yeast cells automatically change sexes—or mating types—every few cell divisions. Animals derive from protists, microbes with nuclei whose vast cellular sexual experimentation holds important clues for the reconstruction of the earliest systems of mating.

Although teleology—the idea that organisms are evolving for a purpose, toward an end—has been widely discredited in evolutionary theory, the idea that sex is retained by evolution and hence must be *for* something continues to plague biological science. But, contrary to academic belief, sex may have *no* evolutionary purpose. We believe, in contrast to many biologists, that sex is chiefly an extraordinary *legacy* of life with its roots in the microcosm. It exists "because" it existed, and now many forms of life are addicted to sex at the core of their biological being: they cannot survive, reproduce, or evolve without it. Human sex is just one example of thirty million or more kinds of sex.

Biologically sex is defined as the process that produces a new individual, a genetically distinct entity derived from more than a single parent. Bacterial sex must be rigorously distinguished from the sex of protists or any other being composed of the more complicated cells with nuclei. Bacteria, sole inhabitants of the Earth for fully 80 percent of its history, have sex lives that differ radically from those of protists, fungi, animals, and plants. Understanding the origins of sex—the scenario of events that led to gene-transfer sex in bacteria and those leading later to the embrace and fusion of protist cells—is a different task from understanding why two-parent sex persists in so many animals and plants. Why haven't more animals, like the all-female whiptail lizards, and more plants, like the prolific dandelions, lost two-parent sex? Why, once animals evolved sexual reproduction, did they not revert (like rotifers and C. *uniparens* lizards) to the "less costly," more rapid, single-parent reproductive mode? Why don't all plants grow from prodigious female parents capable of setting seed in the absence of a pollen-providing male parent?

Many have brought forth attempts to resolve the mystery of "what maintains sex?" We think that the question itself, "Why sex?" is misleading. Samuel Beckett, in one of his plays, writes, "The sun, having no alternative, rose this morning." Animals and plants—sexually reproducing organisms from their inception—remain sexual because they must develop from embryos into animals and plants: like the sun, they lack alternatives. Mammals such as *Homo sapiens* and flowering plants such as poppies remain sexual because they develop from embryos. Embryos each must form from sexual fusion. An ancient sexual legacy from microscopic beings, the animal embryo forms when a male sperm head penetrates a female egg; the young seed forms around the plant embryo in the depths of the flower after pollen delivers the male sperm nucleus to the egg of the female nucleus in the embryo sac. Rarely, plants and animals revert to an asexual mode but it is never complete. Variations on an odd history—one bequeathed from the 1500-million-years-old amoebalike cells—locks both people and poppies into the sexual reproductive mode.

The Peculiar Protists

Human courtship and lovemaking elaborate an essentially purposeless but developmentally essential two-billion-year-old survival "dance"—the doubling up of chromosomes in fertilization and the reduction of the number of those chromosomes in meiosis. In animal development, after the fertilized cells form a body, some of these body cells divide in the male to make sperm, or in the female to form eggs. The microscopically "choreographed" process known as meiosis appears to occur in the cellular depths of all animals. Meiotic sex, which differs greatly from the rampant sex of bacteria, began in protists, the first microscopic beings with nuclei. These forerunners to animal cells structurally resemble cells in human and other animal bodies. The first protists themselves evolved from the intermingling of different kinds of bacteria—symbiotic adventures in which three or four types of bacteria ultimately became completely interdependent, mixing traits like miniature sphinxes and minotaurs, shuffling metabolisms and powers as gracefully as the bodies of chimeras and griffins recombine the limbs of eagles and lions—with the exception that the bacterial mergers have been genetically confirmed as evolutionary fact, while the chimeric beasts proliferate only in the more nebulous realm of the human imagination.

Symbiosis, the living in prolonged physical contact of different kinds of organisms, is a basis of all protist, plant, animal, and fungal life. Animal cells did not evolve directly from bacterial cells that grew large—rather they evolved from bacterial symbiotic mergers. Just as a computer is not a large slide rule but a machine that combines electrical, solid state, mechanical, and television technologies, animal cells have a mixed and complex history. Animal cells evolved as natural selection worked on certain lines of protists. Protists came from symbiotic mergers of once-distinct types of respiring, fermenting, and wriggling bacteria. Plant cells, except for their chloroplasts, inherited separately from photosynthetic green-colored, oxygen-producing bacteria, have the same ancestry as animal cells.

Even in the narrowly biological sense "sex" has myriads of components: cutting and patching of DNA strands (recombination), merging of cells (fertilization), fusing of bodies (copulation), development of gender (differentiation), recognition of the availability of contrasting genders (hormone-based physiology of attraction), and so forth. Jumping genes, "redundant" DNA, nucleotide repair systems, and many other dynamic genetic processes exploit the "cut and paste" recombination of ancient bacteria-style sexuality that evolved long before plants, animals, or even fungi or protists appeared on this planet Earth. Since it is no single question, no *single* answer to the question

"Why sex?" exists. Biologically, sex as the pooling of two genetic systems each with its own DNA nucleotide strands to form a genetically distinct individual is an unkickable genetic habit. Just as the bodies of animals are still composed of organic compounds that were prevalent in the hydrogen-rich atmosphere of Earth during its origin in the young solar system, so mammalian life cycles still depend upon the wet, sensitive behaviors characteristic of gyrating protists and their flagellated bacterial predecessors. Humans indulge in the damp melee not because sex itself is the biological be-all and end-all providing some invaluable evolutionary benefit, but simply because throughout our history, our animal ancestors had no other way to reproduce. In vitro or test-tube fertilization still requires the male's ejaculation and the incubation of the woman's fertile egg in a warm, wet, human womb. Even if some links between intercourse and birth are sundered, for example by human cloning, it will be a long time—probably never—until all connections to the fertile protist and bacterial past are obliterated.

If cloning—making test-tube twins, identical genetic copies—in humans were a practicable form of reproduction, it would, no doubt, be used: pricking a finger you might watch a sped-up film of the blood droplet differentiating into your identical twin. Curiosity might be accompanied by a confusing reevaluation of the self and one's feelings for it, if not an ego rush and digital pleasure. Sex as the formation of individuals with genes from more than a single parent first appeared in promiscuous bacteria, but not until the evolution of protists did sex become necessary, at least in some lineages, for reproduction. We, of course, come from such a protist lineage. Nonetheless, most biological discourse on sex's origin and evolution today usually ignores these little-known cells with nuclei in which meiotic sex both arose and evolved. The nucleated cell itself, parent to the plant and animal cell, evolved when different types of bacteria first attacked and infected, then became chemically enslaved to each other as they organized into new entities. These new entities were the protists, the unicellular prototype of all plant and animal life.

Protist ancestors of the damp sperm and eggs of plants and animals thus have a highly exotic history—they are microscopic sphinxes, come from the permanent mingling of very different kinds of bacteria.

Protists are the smaller members of the great kingdom of life, the Protoctista. First recognized in the mid-nineteenth century to vastly differ from animals and plants by German biologist Ernst Haeckel and named Protoctista by the Scot John Hogg in 1861, this recently reestablished kingdom includes all amoebae, water molds, ciliates, red-tide organisms, slime molds, red, brown, and green seaweeds, and a huge miscellany of other single and multicellular organisms. Their ungainly name is certainly belied by the spectacular appearance of the jewellike pennate diatoms and the beautifully symmetrical radiolarians.

Even now protoctists are erroneously forced to be either animals or plants. Called "protozoa" by tropical physicians and parasitologists who study the few that cause tropical diseases such as sleeping sickness and malaria, they are considered algae by environmental scientists. In spite of terminological malaise, algae, protozoa, slime molds, and other aquatic organisms form a natural group—some 200 thousand species in the Kingdom Protoctista. These organisms predate the Kingdom Animalia and the Kingdom Plantae: neither botanical nor zoological, protoctists are not only harmless but ecologically essential. Furthermore they are "living fossils" of a time of rampant cellular sexual experimentation. The animal-style meiotic sex, the chromosomal dance of cells with nuclei, began in this group, which includes our minute sexual ancestors. As Australian biologist Simon Robson put it, "It would seem that from a vertebrate viewpoint, with regards to the question of the origin of sex, we have been looking at a data set that is three billion years out of date."[1]

Charles Darwin underlined the importance of unusual organisms and their behaviors in the study of evolution. His "oddities and peculiarities" reveal that evolution never plans ahead, but, like a resourceful cobbler, evolution adds and adjusts in fashioning the new. Oddities such as the flightless wings of the penguin are like ashtrays in airplanes that no longer permit smoking at any time. Blind-alley organs, functionless eyes, male nipples, and so forth alert us to historical happenstances—clues to reconstructing the crooked course of evolutionary history. Evolution's quirks include our functionally superfluous fifth toes, which as the hindlimb digits of our monkey ancestors were crucial for grasping tree limbs; cramped in our shoes these bunioned, flesh-covered, bony bits are amusing leftovers of a specific, if arbitrary, past. Other oddities and peculiarities include certain fish jawbones that became the ear bones in reptiles and mammals; and the bladder, the uterus, and the colon, which were a single common organ (the cloaca) in our mammallike reptilian ancestors. Stephen Jay Gould's paradigm example, the panda's "thumb," is really a modified wristbone beyond the fifth finger of the great Chinese black-and-white "bear"—a bony protuberance, it evolved in bamboo-stripping animals later than and entirely separately from the thumb of our primate ancestors. As Gould writes, "Darwin answers that we must look for imperfections and oddities, because any perfection in organic design or ecology obliterates the paths of history. . . . This principle of imperfections became Darwin's most common guide. . . . I like to call it the 'panda principle.' "[2] To find our way to the origins of sex, we apply the panda principle to protists, whose lifestyles are indeed peculiar and odd. Assuming that many microbeings retained their lifestyles from far earlier times, they provide a living library of sexual diversity. Amid this diversity seem to be the very steps that led to the meiotic sex of protoctists and its contemporary offshoot, sexual processes occurring automatically in the cellular depths of human beings.

The Garden of Cleveland

In 1934 the biologist Lemuel Roscoe Cleveland from Harvard University gazed inquisitively at some wood-eating cockroaches in an infested fallen log outside the doorstep of his cabin at the biological station of Mountain Lake, Virginia. That summer Cleveland began an intense study lasting until his death in 1969. He became acquainted with the rich and varied inhabitants of cockroaches and other wood-eating insects such as termites. In the swollen rear intestine of these large Virginia roaches he discovered a sealed world of protists living with almost no oxygen. Swarming inside were squirming corkscrew-shaped bacteria called spirochetes. Still-tinier rod bacteria dwelled and reproduced in even larger numbers. And Cleveland saw that among this entourage were "giant" cells almost half-a-millimeter in length, looming over the smaller creatures like an aircraft carrier or giant submarine.

The environment inside the intestines of Cleveland's wood-eating cockroaches and termites resembles the muddy sea-shores and riverbanks of Earth as they would have appeared to an observer living some 2000 million years ago. Prior to animals or plants, microbes were the only life form. Atmospheric oxygen was negligible, present only in minute quantities near the surfaces of the slimy blue green bacteria that emitted it. The protists and bacteria inside insect intestines are throwbacks to those that swam on moist soils of lakes or seashore muds in the oxygen-reduced planetary environment of the Proterozoic eon, 2500 to 580 million years ago. Eaten, along with algae, bacterial slime, and mud, these minute swimmers resisted the digestive fluids of the paleoinsects that devoured them. By hijacking or stowing away inside the bodies of insects, they retained habitats that remained rich in food and low in oxygen. The microbial stowaways never adapted to the oxygen gas first produced by cyanobacterial ancestors to the chloroplasts of the leaves of grass. Locked in a time capsule, they preserve the era when meiotic sex began.

A microbial voyeur, Cleveland filmed the sex lives of these beings, their gyrations and mergings. He recorded crowds of squiggling, coiling spirochetes swimming together, touching each other, and, sometimes, oscillating in eerie unison. Inside the termite hindgut, bacteria stream in and out of protists. Bacteria excrete and feed, fouling their own nest, but also cleaning it, because the waste of one kind of microbe is often enough food for a different kind. In nature, microbes team up in complex communities to accomplish tasks beyond the ken of any isolated type. They do metabolic work on a global scale, running biospheric processes and completing geochemical cycles crucial to planetary ecology. Such teamwork also occurs in the far more modest realm of the insect hindgut. Wood, undigestable by any single kind, yields enough sugars and organic acids when the persistent microbes interact. The hungry termites ingest the wood and break it into chips. Swimming in the intestine large protists take up the splintered crumbs through their hind ends. They break wood down into cellulose, a food for some bacteria that convert it to sugars and smaller two-carbon compounds that then cross the intestinal wall to feed the termite or roach that shelters all of them.

One of Cleveland's silent film clips depicts an orgiastic chain of three overexcited protists attempting to mate at once. The ceaseless activities within the insect calls up images of New York's Grand Central Station at rush hour. For as long as the termite is alive, the microbes teem and seethe, sleeplessly decomposing and degrading the wood once cropped by the termite's jaws. And the microbes not only dwell in the termite, they are part of it, its lifeblood: a sure sign of imminent death of the insect is the disappearance, up to a week or two earlier, of its intestinal swarms. Elder termites insert gobs of mucousy material, containing a start-up kit of thousands of microbes, into the rear ends of newly hatched termites. This curious rite of protoctist proctology makes sense: without the anal placement of wood digesters, the young termites would die of starvation.

Hours of peering down the microscope confirmed that the microbeasts fed not only on bits of wood-derived cellulose, but when stressed, on each other. This cannibalism intrigued Cleveland. Closely watching a nervous protist cell (called a hypermastigote, or "hairyman," because of the many waving strands of cilia trailing from its sides), he saw the creature engulf its comrade. The swallowed hypermastigote was not fully digested. Muddled and hungry, the engorging host may have considered its half-alive food guest part of itself. Soon the two struggling protists merged; their nuclei fused. This strange event captivated him: had he just been witness to a latter-day version of the very events that, more than a 1000 million years earlier, led to the first fertilization? In meiotic sex, cells that have halved their chromosome numbers by meiosis to become eggs and sperm then merge—you know how—to regain their lost number. In the primordial ooze, merging would have happened not from sexual urges but simply to allay a terrible thirst and a primordial starvation. The peculiar sort of doubling and partial digestion Cleveland witnessed in his laboratory provided a living testimony of the Proterozoic past. The protists that ate each other in the laboratory belonged to the same species. The first fertilization event on the early Earth could have been a similar act of "cannibalism."

Human fertilization occurs in the abdomen of a woman when a man's tiny numerous sperm encounter a relatively large single egg in her fallopian tube. The first sexually reproducing organisms, however, were probably more like modern protists such as the green alga *Chlamydomonas* or the ciliate *Paramecium*, in which the entire protist body is a single cell. The body itself is a germ or sex cell pushing for procreation; these genderless cells, equal in size, are indistinguishable. Attracted to each other they stick together and mate.

The primeval participants in meiotic sex may have been forced by hunger or thirst to merge. Did life's two most sensual thrills, the joys of food and sex, at one time satisfy a single desire? Fascinatingly, there is evidence that these two most epicurean delights once fulfilled the same hunger: biologists today who wish to induce caniballike sexual mergers do so by applying conditions that seem to mirror the hypothesized ancient environment in which microbial cannibalism may have been the desperate answer to a desperate situation. To study genetic systems *Chlamydomonas* is starved for nitrogen, *Paramecium* deprived of all food, *Spirogyra* cooled or dried out. When thus deprived, these protists are attracted and cling to their potential mates. Indeed, one of the "peculiarities and oddities" of protists like the green alga *Chlamydomonas* and fungi like *Saccharomyces* yeast is that, while reproduction always can be uniparental (asexual), sexual fusion leads to the formation of cysts or spores. These doubled honeymooners form resistant structures able to withstand extended periods of drought and starvation.

Cell fusion or meiotic sex started in moist, dark-dwelling protists lacking mouths, penises, vaginas, stomachs, and anuses. If people displayed the biology of these protists and fungi that periodically fuse, we would have no gender, and our bodies would be neuter. Only after releasing some previous drops of a real aphrodisiac, a protein-containing "sweat," would it be noticed that we came in two kinds. One half of us would secrete a chemical typical of our mating type and the other half would be excited by the secretion. Such chemicals released into the water powerfully attract the members of the opposite mating type who are otherwise indistinguishable. If people were algae, our green, round bodies would exude one of two types of attractants only when we were starving for nitrogen. The aphrodisiac would signal such starvation. After a protracted time during which we would be permitted no meat, no tofu, no legumes—no food containing nitrogen— we would begin to despair. Sugar and starch are food molecules, but they lack nitrogen, an essential ingredient of all proteins and genes. These carbohydrates would repulse us. Nauseated and weakening, if nitrogen still were not somehow supplied, huddled in the water with our equally squalid, green, globular friends, we would either die or fuse. Faced with death you would fuse with any neighbor of the opposite mating type, virtually whomever you could find. Completely merging with your partner you would become part of a doubled monster. The act of doubling would increase your nitrogen to the bare minimum necessary for survival. In this condition as doubled monster you would hold out until spring, or until new sources of nitrogen arrived.

Such an odd lifestyle is typical for many modern day protists. Lacking nitrogen, two cells fuse. Each has a nucleus with only a single set of chromosomes. The whole nucleus of one mating partner then fuses with the nucleus of the second in a further intimacy called karyogamy. The product of the protist sex act now has two of everything—doubled sets of nucleoli, mitochondria, and chloroplasts, and two copies of the chromosomal DNA and its attached proteins. Those protists failing to escape their doubled state will tend to die, especially if, in later dire straits, they triple or quadruple by further merging. By contrast, those that "relieve" themselves from doubleness will tend to survive. But a question then arises: How can the doubled monsters, which derived from primeval acts of cannibalistic merging, return to their streamlined single forms? How can they again become like those first driven to swallow their fellow creatures whole?

Sudden changes of environmental conditions forcing protist cells to die or fuse still occur today in soils, along river banks, in drying pools, and tidal flats. The reverse process, of diploid cells reverting to original haploid cells in the single-chromosomal state, Cleveland took to be the key to the origins of sex. He wrote about the desperate need of doubled cell monsters to be "relieved" of their diploidy. Even though he published his key paper on the origins of meiotic sex in *Science*, nearly no one cited it.[3] His colleagues were not ready to think about the far-reaching implications of protist private lives.

Orgies and Androgynes

Mating in protists does not always proceed, like the beasts marching onto Noah's Ark, two-by-two. Although in no way our direct ancestors, contemporary protoctists such as the ciliate *Sorogena*, the slime mold *Acrasea*, and many amoebomastigotes have positively orgiastic sex lives. When conditions around them become intolerable—when famine or drought sets in—they fuse by the tens or even hundreds of thousands. They swarm and squiggle, recognizing each other. They engage in a massive orgy analogous to fertilization. The result of all the fused cells is, relatively speaking, a giant being. Mistaking food for sex and sex for food, they merge into a moving morass that becomes much more than a doubled or tripled monster. In this evolutionary sideshow of odd sex lives, only those capable of undoing or resolving their state of multiplicity or monstrosity and of returning to a single body have survived until today. And yet each cell in our human body is in such a doubled and monstrous state. We too are oddly coupled, colossal collections, an orgiastic, if organized, intermingling of beings. And the only time *we* come out of our selves into the primordial state of singleness is ever so briefly: in men, when sperm cells are formed in the testes—only to be released during a seminal emission; in fetal girls in the young ovary, where ova are released fifteen to forty years later on a monthly schedule. Except for eggs and sperm we are marked by the doubleness of chromosome sets in each cell of our body.

Since the cellular details of sex vary so profoundly among protoctists, meiotic sex probably evolved many times.[4] The independent ancestry of sexually reproducing beings can be concluded from the differences in the return of each generation to an "uncoupled" state. In humans, this return via meiosis to the single state is inconspicuous and fleeting. Meiosis occurs in the scrotum-covered testes of men throughout their adult lives as they make sperm; in a woman, meiosis occurs only in her ovaries when she herself is in the womb; the female baby is born with eggs already in place. The eggs and sperm of people are reminiscent of the protists ancestral to the entire animal lineage. Unless they are carefully frozen in special preservative solutions, released sperm and eggs do not survive for more than a few hours, or two weeks at most. The imperative of the mature gamete—egg or sperm—is to fuse or die. If they do fuse, the doubled being, the fertilized egg, grows by mitosis—that is, asexual cell reproduction. The cells of the embryo multiply to become the fetus. These, in turn, give rise to the infant, the child, the adolescent, and the adult. At all these later stages each human cell remains in the doubled, diploid state; each bears two sets of genes, the ancient imprint of a doubled ancestry.

The sexual doubling of the billions of nucleated cells in our bodies suggests that we are genetic androgynes, combinations of the two sexes. As individuals we live in a permanently fertilized state; each cell gathers together the "male" and "female" for the duration of our lives. Only the egg and sperm qualify as being distinctly sexed. All the rest of the body cells are hermaphrodites: in a very rational sense we may consider ourselves, by and large, dual-sexed, ambisexual, androgynous, the diploid elaboration of a primordial duality alien only to the still more primordial egg and sperm. And when these last come together, as they so often do, to make a living embryo, the result is worldly reincarnation, a new consciousness, a new "I." Boy or girl, the child emerges as duality; in virtually its entire body, it carries on the legacy of duality inherited from the merging of the two parents' cellular nuclei.

This view of the androgynous human body finds its counterpart in psychology. Freud considered people to be fundamentally bisexual. In developing his analytical psychology, Freud's student Carl Jung veered away from the idea that psychological bisexuality was in any way harmful or pathological. Indeed, for Jung the soul of the man is female, an *anima*, while the soul of the female is male, an *animus*; the nurturing female part of man, largely unconscious, can be inseminated, as it were, by the *logos spermaticos* of the woman's sublimated male soul, her *animus*. Feelings, emotions, in men come from his female *anima*, just as opinions or certainties blossom directly from the woman's unconscious *animus*. Obviously, Jung's formation may be too dichotomous and over-simplified, but the central idea of a single body-mind, or a soma-psyche seems a good one.

Long before the recognition of evolution and the mutability of species, enchanting myths emphasized sexual doubleness. From the Dogon peoples of West Africa, to the Babylonians and Maori, creation has been pictured as an androgynous union or chaotic miasma that settles into the male and the female, into Earth and sky. The sexual intercourse of the two genders thus tends to restage or reunite a primal scene.

One of the most eloquent expressions of sexual doubleness

comes through the lips of Aristophanes in Plato's *Symposium*. At a banquet each guest offers an opinion on the meaning of erotic love. When his turn arrives, Aristophanes refers to the primordial form of humanity, in which men and women were merged into Androgynes. The menwomen, menmen, and womenwomen were permanently mating interlocked spheres with two sets of limbs. Stronger than the mortal men and women of today, the menwomen, menmen, and womenwomen propelled themselves by rolling like wheels or balls. By and by the menwomen, menmen, and womenwomen began to worry Zeus, just as the Titans and the Giants had done. To ward off the danger, as in an operation for Siamese twins, Zeus split the menwomen, menmen, and womenwomen all into separate halves, just as one would "split an egg with a horsehair." Zeus "ordered Apollo to turn the face and the half-neck around towards the cut, so that man, confronted with his cleavage, would become more moral, and the rest he ordered Apollo to heal."[5] Originally, the spheres came in three perfectly matched varieties, gay, lesbian, and hetero. But angry Zeus split us in two and tied the loose ends in a knot at the front. This was the navel. In a second operation genitals were moved around to the front. "Thereupon Zeus took pity and placed another means at their disposal, by shifting their private parts to the front, instead of on the side where they were before, since previously they had reproduced not in one another but in the earth, like crickets. Now, however, he shifted them to the front and thus allowed them to reproduce one another."[6] The result, of course, was men and women. Humans no longer posed a threat. Today our separate halves wander the Earth, restlessly but unsuccessfully seeking union. And the clowning Aristophanes reminds us that Zeus may split us again if we don't keep still: "quartered," with half a face, we will hop around on one leg, like a top.

The protist cannibals—like those observed by L. R. Cleveland—are a living, real version of Aristophanes's adrogynes: the primordial spheres in a doubled state. However tiny, our ancestors may have been just such monstrous combinations, more powerful than their single counterparts in extracting nitrogen and in surviving without water or food. They were not split by a horsehair but naturally in the process of meiotic cell division. Since then our bodies retained the urgency of their protistan ancestors. When man and woman join in sexual ecstasy they come out of themselves, warm and wet in the reestablishment of their primordial state as merged cells that preceded their existence. Whether this act has ultimate meaning is questionable. It is less a noble tragedy than a comedy of errors, condemned to repetition. Perhaps the universe is an organic dance, a play of appearances behind which there are only other appearances; the cosmic equivalent of a masked ball; in which case, the unification of parental genes to make the unique genome of a new person is as ingenious as it is ingenuous; it is generous in that it gives new life but pathological in that it sabotages the integrity of the paternal organization, the originality of the original genomes. Sexuality gently shakes us up. Then not so gently. It rattles our identity, and the ground of our conceptions, with all the crazy force of a hissing locomotive train.

Why Sex Remains

Iago, in Shakespeare's *Othello*, scoffed at those who considered sex sublime. For Iago it was all "goats and monkeys"—a kind of brute animal necessity revealing kinship with the lowly beasts. But beyond even goats and monkeys, birds and bees, is Cleveland's garden of microbes, the organisms in which sex as fertilization first began. And beyond them are the minute bacteria from whose genetic engineering processes all subsequent life derived. In nonancestral protists, sex is not only not reproduction but it is not even correlated with survival. *Stentor coeruleus* is an unusual protist with a sexual legacy quite different from our own. These ciliates are bizarre: whenever *Stentor* partners couple, both inevitably die. Needless to say, *Stentor*'s usual procedure is to reproduce asexually and live. About once a year in spring, as days grow longer, two *Stentor* atavistically attempt sexual union. They lock together in a thirty-six-hour-long embrace; meiotic nuclei begin to flow from genderless mate to genderless mate. But the romance, as always in these beings, is a lethal mistake. In each case, within three to four days after separating, the microbes die. Apparently each *Stentor* receives from the other a set of nuclei that destroys the ability not only to reproduce but to live at all.

The example of *Stentor* makes us wonder why, even after desperate organisms had become sexual reproducers, they would remain so. Isn't all the effort involved in finding a mate, chemically attracting it, and compromising with it long enough for sexual interchange more complex than simple one-parent reproduction? In *Hippolytus*, a rarely performed play by Euripides, Hippolytus, a worshipper of chastity, rails against Woman. The occasion is the absence of his father, during which his ill-advised stepmother admits she is hopelessly in love with him, her own stepson. In a monologue Hippolytus demands of Zeus why he made women. If you wanted us poor mortals to produce offspring, Hippolytus cries, why did you not simply allow us to *purchase* them?

The argument for the superfluousness of the opposite sex still exists, although now it is more often used to indict men. Serious biology books such as *The Redundant Male* and *Why Males Exist* as well as magazine and newspaper articles with titles such as "Why Sex?" alert us to academia's focus not on sexuality's origins but on its maintenance.[7] If sexual organisms—females anyway—are able to reproduce perfectly well, without the energetic bother of encountering, pairing, joining together each generation, why do sexual organisms remain sexual? Don't bacteria, amoebae, duckweed, whiptails, and other asexual beings reproduce much more efficiently and faster than sexual organisms? Shouldn't all parthenogenetic animals, mothers bearing only daughters, eventually supplant sexually reproducing species with males and fathers? Shouldn't males become entirely redundant? Lost with disuse?

The evidence of natural history is that sexually reproducing

species are widely spread. Despite the advantages of speed and
ease accruing to members of nonsexually reproducing species,
what *maintains* so many far-flung sexual species? What are
the continuing advantages for these species? The traditional
textbook explanation, buttressed by the mathematical analyses
of population biologists such as Ronald A. Fisher and, later,
George C. Williams, was that by combining genes, sexually
reproducing species or organisms enjoyed a potential advantage
over asexual ones in changing environments. Assuming that
sexual organisms show more variation, and noticing that some
plant and animal populations such as the rotifer *Euchlanis
dilatata* can reproduce either with or without sex, Williams
compares the persistence of sexual reproduction to a lottery in
which winning numbers are continually changed. Asexual
organisms, like gamblers who buy tickets with numbers that
have won in the past but will not necessarily win again, lose
out despite buying a huge number of tickets. Natural selection,
in this view, has not produced a world of virgin mothers and
daughters, unmolested by the time-consuming rigamarole
mandated by men and sex, because sex adds genetic variety.
Females produce the offspring; they hypothetically could reproduce without males, but they do not because in rapidly
changing environments and under intense selection some of
them get just the genes they need from males with unusual,
now useful, traits.

There are difficulties with this view. First, according to
Williams' own calculations, sexual forms would only be maintained under conditions of intense sibling competition and
crowding that long-lived, mobile and sexual species manage
in the real world. Thus the lottery explanation works better
for organisms such as oysters, aphids, and elm trees than it
does for mobile, slowly-reproducing organisms such as elephants.[8] In general, simply because some species such as *Euchlanis dilatata* can reproduce both sexually and asexually does
not mean that, once established, sex is easily lost. Once entrenched, two-parent sex is difficult to escape. No animal or
plant has lost all processes associated with it. The cellular dance
of meiosis (or at least that early stage of it when the chro-

mosomes pair up—"meiotic prophase I") as well as cell fusion, continue to exist even in parthenogenetic animals.

At the cellular level parthenogenetic animals have not lost sex, they just perform it with themselves. Although strictly daughter-producing species of fish, lizards, and rotifers exist, meiotic prophase, in which the chromosomes undergo DNA repair along with special protein or RNA syntheses, seems to be indispensable to the lives of these animals. Animal-style meiotic sex embeds itself. Apparently the habit of meiosis, with its complex synthetic machinations, especially DNA repair, and the fusion of haploids, has never been "kicked" in beings that maintain complex tissue differentiation, and this includes all animals and plants. Therefore "sexually reproducing animals and plants" and not "sexual reproduction" is what natural selection has maintained.

Offspring of only a single parent are not, as is commonly believed, identical. They show much variation. A "parent" is not a single, stable entity. It is not even a single organism. Animals and plants contain millions of microbes on and in their bodies. Plant and animal cells harbor viruses and millions of other roving genetic fragments. Far from "pure," every plant and animal cell is "heterogenomic," marked by an ancient miscegenation between bacteria of different species, bacteria whose genomes had to interact and partially merge before plants, animals, or even protists evolved in the first place. The parent, though it may reproduce asexually, is already a genetic morass.

The problem with the traditional explanation of why organisms remain sexual in populations is that, counter to widespread assumption, sex is not needed to produce inherited variation upon which natural selection must act. Variation sufficiency can be compared with the amount of sexual intercourse in a population required to generate sufficient human offspring. A promiscuous animal might have fewer offspring than one less sexually active; just as, beyond a minimal frequency, sexual intercourse becomes redundant for the purposes of generating offspring, so, beyond a certain quantity, genetic variety is redundant for the purposes of natural selection. Closely related single-parent and biparental organisms both show considerable amounts of variation; many species of fungi, leguminous plants, and cloned tomato cells, for example, lack two-parent sex yet show enormous variation from parent to offspring. The concept, long touted by textbooks, that sex is maintained because sexual organisms, which are presumably more varied, can adapt faster to changing environments, has not been borne out by observations. To the surprise of many biologists, uniparental fatherless rotifers and lizards can be just as varying and evolutionarily successful as their biparental counterparts. The assumption that asexual organisms lack sufficient variation to adapt to rapidly changing environments fails. Sex is *not* primarily a method for generating evolutionary variation; many other methods exist.

The question of how meiotic sex *originated* differs from the question of how meiotic sex is actively maintained. The origins of meiotic sex are traced to thriving cannibalistic protists, but what accounts for its persistence? Fisher first proposed that, because sex distracted from the business of reproducing, it was bad for individuals; it was preserved because it was good for species. Sexual species, he claimed, diversified into new forms, whereas asexual species, their members all adapted to a single environment, foundered and became extinct during times of rapid environmental change. G. C. Williams flipped this concept around, paradoxically suggesting that sexual species are maintained because they are poorly adapted, their constant shuffling of genes preventing them from specializing to a particular niche that would make them extinct if it disappeared. Sexual organisms evolve faster because with two sets of genes they are protected from deleterious mutations by complementary good genes, claimed *Drosophila* (fruit fly) geneticist H. J. Muller. Potentially useful genetic traits could be kept latent in a population, disappearing only if so many mutations accumulated at once that they killed their bearers and thus were effectively dumped from the gene pool all at the same time. In asexual organisms, however, lethal mutations could never be masked by good genes or salvaged for their possible helpful uses with other combinations of genes in the future.

Leigh Van Valen, professor of evolutionary biology at the University of Chicago, invokes still another reason for sexual maintenance, which he calls the "Red Queen" hypothesis, named after the character in *Alice in Wonderland* who said, "It takes all the running you can do, to keep in the same place." The Red Queen hypothesis states that once sex evolves, the environment, consisting largely of other organisms, jumps to a state of more rapid change. From this vantage point an environment such as the rain forest of the Amazon river basin, with its impressive diversity of interacting species, may be understood as an example of runaway sexual evolution. If asexual organisms have insufficient recourse to sources of genetic variation, they will be left behind, adapted only to the less dynamic environments of the past. Robert Trivers believes biotic interactions may be crucial to understanding sex, since the evolution of a species' predators, prey, and parasites calls for the sort of counter-evolution facilitated by sexual recombination; Trivers suggests that sex, like dispersal, is a means of escaping rapidly evolving parasites. On a more neutral note with regard to its adaptive advantage, Dr. Richard E. Michod of the University of Arizona believes biparental sex is maintained as a method of repairing damaged genes. "Males," he says, "are a way of providing redundant information. When females are damaged, they can use information from males to repair their bad genes."

These theories for maintenance of sex all share an unstated assumption: that sex confers some evolutionary advantage. But does it? What is the advantage of the redness of mammalian blood—is there one, or is the color red just a neutral legacy of the ability of the hemoglobin in it to carry oxygen? "What maintains sex?" also may be a poor question. The persistence of their bizarre ritual of mating and dying suggests that protists such as *Stentor* used to survive sexual encounters. But since death inevitably results from mating, sexuality in *Stentor* may be an atavism, a lingering attachment to a once-adaptive form of behavior that is now deadly, a disability of evolutionary momentum similar to our taste for territorial warfare in an age of globally dispersed nuclear weapons.

Mammalian sexual reproduction is far more a nexus of evolutionary momentum, a knot or web of deeply entangled, prehistorically intertwined features. Intrinsically involving an egg stimulated by a sperm that develops into an embryo prior to the fetus, youth, and adulthood, sexual reproduction is impossible to purge in modern mammals. In complex and orchestrated cell collectives such as mammals the entire story of development begins with the irreducibly sexual event of spermatic attraction to and penetration of the egg. DNA repair during meiosis, the process that pares down cells to make these sperm and eggs, may pave the way for the formation of an embryo. If so, sex, at the cellular level, is not dispensable without dispensing with the life cycle itself. Sex at the cellular level is far more difficult to purge than the skin-to-skin shenanigans of lovers, who already, thanks to laboratory glassware fertilization techniques, never even need to see each other to reproduce. The molecular heart of mammalian sex is far older and more refractory. Sex is not the tragic flaw of human heroes, but rather the repeated errancy of evolutionary beings, warm, wet flesh destined to repeat the past even as it learns the secret that this flesh is fundamentally illogical and repetitive, a kind of stuttering mineral. Meiotic sex is a detour, a beautiful accident. It is like a thread caught on the cogwheel of reproduction that cannot now be dismantled without damage to the whole whirring apparatus. Life goes on.

Mathematically, ridding organisms of meiotic sex is as easy as dropping a variable. In reality, purging the life cycle of meiotic sex is as easy as bypassing childhood, eliminating an animal's blood, or removing electricity from Tokyo or New York City.

Bacterial Sex Lives

Bacterial sex probably arose over 3500 million years ago on an Earth that would have smelled like a latrine, an Earth whose atmosphere lacked oxygen and ozone, an Earth continuously bombarded by ultraviolet radiation from space. If you had been around to smell the Archean Earth, the preponderance of atmospheric gases such as ammonia, sulfide, and hydrocarbons would have wrinkled your nose with their primordial stink. But nobody could have smelled the funky early Earth in which the earliest sex began: the planet three billion years ago was anaerobic; it lacked an oxygen atmosphere. Oxygen only accumulated in the atmosphere when bacterial mutants discovered water as a source of hydrogen in photosynthesis. As these early mutant precursors to plants grew, they gave off oxygen as waste. Eventually enough oxygen gathered to create a shield of ozone, an invisible atmosphere blanket that blocked ultraviolet rays and slowed down the rates of death and DNA damage to the bacteria dwelling at the surface. Sex evolved before the ozone layer appeared, and although some suggest that sex may even have evolved in unstable molecules before the origin of life, we believe it probably began in bacteria who were genetically mutilated by solar radiation. When these bacteria found ways to replace their damaged DNA with imported DNA, with DNA outside their bodies, that was the first sex. Bacterial sex began on a planet that would seem a little enchanted and alien. Without green plants or animals or fresh air it was a hotter, more dramatic planet, circling a star dimmer than the sun we know today and with a swifter period of rotation causing shorter nights and days. We ourselves are souvenirs of this energetic, volcanic world whose carbon- and hydrogen-rich chemical compounds are no longer found in the environment. Like reproducing chunks of a magically preserved foreign world, the funky stuff lingers on, housed and protected in the good old form of our bodies, of the bodies of all modern-day organisms. Organisms all of which have descended from the chemically most diverse, genetically most promiscuous, and environmentally most ancient beings on the planet: the bacteria.

Today, in nature, bacteria continuously feed on, attach to, and some even interpenetrate each other; living in dense collectives, under the widest variety of conditions, they continue to trade their genes. The famous "genetic recombination" of molecular biology demonstrates that parts of bacteria continue to roam, that genetic interchange occurs not only *between* but *within* organisms. Embryology, epigenesis, ontogeny—the whole adventure of individual growth from fertile egg to sexually mature adult—is a kind of ecological self-organization of social bacteria.

A sexual being, by biologists' definition, has at least two parents; and "gender" refers to the differences between these two parents. If bacteria have "genders" they are very subtle. Conjugating bacteria, before conjugation, look and behave just like each other. During conjugation, though, the rounded form, the "male" bacterium with a "fertility factor" among "his" genes, injects DNA into a "female" recipient whose DNA lacks fertility factor genes. In this travesty of transvestism, the "female," owing to its possession of the fertility factor, now becomes "male." The genetic gift can be passed on, indefinitely, changing genders as it goes.

Sex, as bacterial conjugation, began long before the first animal, plant, fungus, or protist. Although textbooks speak of the two offspring of a dividing bacterium as "daughter cells," dividing bacteria are in fact neither male nor female; unless confronted with sexual opportunity they are, for all practical purposes, genderless. To reproduce, bacteria do not need, as people do, to give or receive the genes of any sexual partner. Bacteria not only reproduce routinely by direct division, without any sex at all, but during sex they give or receive any number of genes. Bacteria-style sexuality in this way is more advanced than our own. Stretches of DNA—genes—move from one bacterium to another. If naked and uncoated they are called plasmids; by contrast, protein-coated bits of DNA— "clothed" genes—are known as viruses or phages.

Bacterial cells donate and receive genes in the form of plasmids and viruses all the time. Unlike plants or animals that are limited to sex with members of their own species, one kind of bacterium can pass on genes to a second kind that greatly differs from it. Contrasting the fluid promiscuity of bacterial genetic exchange with animal sex involving mating, fertilization, and meiosis, biology professor Betsey Dexter Dyer of Wheaton College claims that bacteria indulge in "advanced sex." Such sex, for example, took place between a *Gonococcus* bacterium and a different penicillin-resistant bacterium in the human lower gut or colon where many bacteria thrive. A new gonorrhea-producing strain of spherical gonococci now resistant to the penicillin antibiotic resulted. The very possibility of "genetic recombination" and "molecular biology" depends on this advanced sex of bacteria.

When exposed to ultraviolet radiation, many types of bacteria burst open to release bacteriophages, tiny bacterial viruses each carrying a set of genes including those from the bacteria in which they used to reside. These bacteriophages soon hook up to the surface of other bacteria. They inject their own genes as well as those carried from their previous bacterial encounter, inside new bacteria. In this way, viruses send genetic messengers around the microbial world.

Because they trade genes so promiscuously, bacteria transcend the traditional species boundaries. Indeed, if a "species" is defined as that group of organisms whose members interbreed, then only a single species of bacterium exists on Earth.

Solar radiation may have caused the first bacterial sex some four billion years ago. Solar radiation contains ultraviolet light, which damages DNA. And yet until two billion years ago no ozone layer—which prevents ultraviolet light from penetrating the atmosphere to damage life on the surface of the Earth—even existed. Without an ozone layer, therefore, ultraviolet damage was even worse in the remote past. Some of this vast damage was repaired by enzymes; DNA-making and -repairing enzymes detect and fix broken ends of DNA. Such DNA repair requires the use of fresh, undamaged, unirradiated DNA. This pristine DNA may come from a neighboring virus, phage, or bacterium. And the first time a bacterium patched its wounded DNA by borrowing undamaged DNA from a fresh source we have an event that qualifies as the origin of sex.

A remarkable discovery of molecular biology is that of transposons—small bits of DNA that travel. Transposons residing in a cell may be copied and moved elsewhere in that same cell, or to other cells or even to other organisms. Genetic engineering, the profitable laboratory technique of introducing bits of DNA from one organism into another to confer new heritable traits, is really a human reworking of naturally occurring bacterial maneuvers. This global interchange of genetic material, an all-natural biotechnology billions of years old, is the legacy of sexuality in bacteria. If people ever learn to genetically engineer themselves to grow cranial horns, leopard-spotted skin, or other attributes first fashionable in the animal world, it will be thanks to genetic recombination, which is to say by the grace of advanced bacterial sex.

Nakedness

Theodosius Dobzhansky, the great Russian evolutionist who lived the last part of his life in the United States, said, "Nothing in biology makes sense except in the light of evolution."[9] We need not be "genetic determinists," sociobiologists, or neo-Darwinists to recognize the deep truth of Dobzhansky's insight. The biology of all of us is, of course, molded, mollified, suppressed, expanded, nurtured, denied, and altered in various ways by the overwhelming importance of society and culture. But, in spite of our articulate, evasive, and "well-reasoned" arguments to the contrary, for no length of time can we overcome, bypass, transcend, or ignore our living nature. Living membrane-bounded cells evolved from complex interactions in the supernovae of stars through interactions of carbon-hydrogen chemicals with solar energy. Cells are life's fundamental units, which, supplying themselves with water, food, and energy, cannot help but grow and reproduce. Expansion, chemical transformation, and reproduction—these are the ways of all life.

Many mechanisms integrate collections of cells and make them more than just cells. Integrated collections of cells on the early Earth passed their genes back and forth in a frenzy of bacterial promiscuity; they become swimming protists that evolved into organisms with tissues, organisms such as toads and papayas. Some of these cell communities hardened into trees. Integrated collections of different bacterial cell types became the protist ancestors to animal and plant cell life. They also, under the right conditions and with rich allotments of energy and time, transformed into mountains of limestone and deposits of iron ore. Certain types of protist cells, bound together through millions of years, became animals; yet, still in each generation, these animals reduced back to female ovum and male sperm. Animals bound together through millions of years became colonies, societies, packs, and herds. Cannibalism became fertilization and meiosis was forced to evolve. Animal interactions led to discrete life forms larger and perhaps more complex than any single animal, to reef corals, brachiopod colonies, to human tribes that led to villages that became sky-sprawling cities. Sexual and parasexual processes led to cell motility and cell recognition. Cell binding, cell fusion, DNA get-together leading to gene fusions followed. Fungi attacked but could not destroy their algal food and lichens were forced to evolve. Grass-eating mammals ingested undigestible soil microbes, ciliates, and bacteria that digested the cellulose of grass for them; cows evolved. Sex, on the biochemical level in the broad sense of the formation of a new organism with genes from more than a single parent, has been with life—in one or another of its guises—from the beginning of its residence on Earth.

Nearly four billion years after Earth's origin, we, like all other of the eight thousand or so species of mammals, but unlike all other thirty million or more living species on Earth today, are milk-sucking, hairy beings, essentially four-legged and five-fingered, capable of retaining nearly constant body temperature. Unlike many other organisms on Earth, we mammals absolutely require sexual conception for our very existence and for the proliferation of our descendants. Unlike nearly all other organisms on Earth we produce helpless new infants who absolutely require careful and continuous adult affection and nurturance. Unlike nearly all other earthly beings, too, we crave narrative—we lust for a beginning, a middle, and an end. We want the story of life. We yearn to understand the sexuality that, adding its immortal spice, enhances and limits our lives. We want to be sure, to know in both the carnal and the cognitive sense. But carnal knowledge remains oxymoronic, elusive, tantalizingly unsatisfactory as it promises more than it can give, ensuring desire as it brings us one step closer to the still greater enigma of death. It is as if the evolutionary stripteaser were twisting, turning her paper back on humanity and moving on, inexorably, to the next phase in the endless routine.

And it is an endless routine. The truth of the evolutionary striptease is not static and unchanging. Instead, it is glimpsed, here and there, always in time, in the flirtatious gestures of a show. The happening of truth, as Heidegger says, always occurs in the context of untruth, just as lighting and clarity are recognized only in relation to darkness and obscurity. Confronted with the stripper's final unveiling we witness a kind of dissolution—the incestuous dissolving of his body back into Earth, a final merging of cells. The Greek word *aletheia*—traditionally translated as "truth"—contains *lethe*, meaning hiding or securing, within it. For Heidegger truth as aletheia is the movement into unconcealment, a kind of unsecuring or revealing that always retains internal ties to veiling and security. If this is wordplay it is wordplay that describes the almost infinite jesting—the "dancing on the feet of chance" as Nietzsche put it—of material reality itself. Etymologically, our word "measure"—such an important concept and practice in modern science—shares roots with the Sanskrit term *maya*, a key word for Hindu philosophy, broadly designating illusion. *Webster's Seventh New Collegiate Dictionary* defines *maya* as "the sense-world of manifold phenomena held in Vedanta to conceal the unity of absolute being; *broadly*: ILLUSION." The play, the dance of censoring senses in *maya* refreshes our sense of the ultimate unrootedness of science, of its dependence upon human values and conceptions. The true story is sought for balance, a base, a firm foothold, or eternal measure. But none is to be found, only a mirage of colorful ground covering a black abyss. The evolutionary striptease is light, high, she dances, tips scales. Her costume is a false cover, a second skin, and her face is a facade beneath a mask of a mask. She becomes a he. They are either side of a neuter monster who demonstrates its wound along the castrated midline of the androgyne. Strictly speaking, the stripper *is* not but is always becoming.

The evolutionary stripper alerts us to contingency of our symbols, language, and metaphors of knowledge. Knowledge is often described as something light, as in the light of reason, something revealed, *dis*-covered, something shown. But the evolutionary stripper provides a humble counterexample: each showy display hides and conceals. No stripper exists except as flimsy garments, paper dress, fishnet stockings of peek-a-boo words. The stripper is ink blots, typewritten signals, a literary device, as insubstantial as those vision-obscuring films of air that spread over the sand on a hot day at the beach. She is no more real than the succubus who, slight of body, rests her head on Reginald Scot's shoulder in the mist of a centuries-old dream.

These chapters elaborated the mystery dance, retracing its steps, detailing a history of human sexuality. Turning to many scientific and literary sources, we tentatively recreated the past. Between these covers, upon these sheets, pen was put to paper in an exploration of female orgasm, of the unconscious mind and body games played by sexually evolving primeval lovers. Reptile holograms mounted each other, like three-dimensional hieroglyphs in a writing ancestral to language. Pages became ages as we gazed at the passage of our ancestors from microbes to amphibians, from floating fish to apes gazing at the irises of their eyes in mirrors. But after it is all over, the problems posed by the evolutionary stripper must be borne in mind. The stripper cannot be separated from the striptease—the dancer cannot be distanced from the dance. The undressing of the stripper is her body, the removal of her cosmetics leaves the cosmos.

S(he) is bottomless. The dance never ends.

Notes
and References

Introduction:
Evolutionary Striptease

1. Scot, Reginald (1538?–1599), 1972. *The Discoverie of Witchcraft*, with an introduction by Montague Summers, Dover Publications, New York.

2. Dinnerstein, Dorothy, 1976. *The Mermaid and the Minotaur: Sexual Arrangements and Human Malaise*, Harper & Row Publishers, New York. In perhaps the most powerful sentence in the book (p. 234), Dinnerstein declares (in response to Freud's famous question, What do women want?): "*What women want is to stop serving as scapegoats* (their own scapegoats as well as men's and children's scapegoats) *for human resentment of the human condition.*"

3. Derrida, Jacques, 1981. *Dissemination* (Barbara Johnson, trans.), University of Chicago Press, Chicago, Illinois.

4. Cited in Allison, David (ed.), 1988. *The New Nietzsche*, MIT Press, Cambridge, Massachusetts, p. 49.

5. MacLean, Paul D., 1978. "Why Brain Research on Lizards?" in *Behavior and Neurology of Lizards* (N. Greenberg and P. D. MacLean, eds.), National Institute of Mental Health, Bethesda, Maryland, p. 5.

6. Kretsinger, Robert H., 1987. In book review of Margulis, L., and Sagan, D., 1986, *Origins of Sex*, Yale University Press, New Haven, Connecticut. *Origins of Life*, 17, p. 209.

7. Cited in Norris, Chirstopher, 1987. *Derrida*, Harvard University Press, Cambridge, Massachusetts, p. 121. What Derrida actually wrote in *Of Grammatology* was "il n'y a pas de hors-texte," which Norris translated as "there is no 'outside' to the text."

8. Lamb, S. M., 1987. In *Semiotics in Education: A Dialogue*, College Press, Claremont, California, p. 21.

I. Sperm Contest

EPIGRAPH: Rumi, Jalaluddin (1207–1273). *Open Secret, Versions of Rumi*, 1984, by John Moyne and Coleman Barks, Threshold Books, Putney, Vermont. Jalaluddin Rumi was a Sufi love mystic who wildly spun around as he delivered his musical verses, which were transcribed by his assistants. He was the first "Whirling Dervish," and it is claimed that his poetry read aloud in the Persian original was so musical it sent listeners into a trance by its aural qualities alone.

1. Harcourt, A. H., and Harvey, Paul H., 1984. "Sperm Competition, Testes Size, and Breeding Systems in Primates," in *Sperm Competition and the Evolution of Animal Mating Sytems*, Robert Smith (ed.), Academic Press, Orlando, Florida, p. 599.

2. The testes tests, done by Robin Baker and Mark Ellis of the University of Manchester, were mentioned by Robert L. Smith during his talk in a session on sperm competition at the 1990 American Association for the Advancement of Science meeting in New Orleans.

3. Shearer, L., September 10, 1978. "Sex Sensation," in *Intelligence Report, Parade Magazine*. And see Smith, R., *Sperm Competition*, pp. 615–16.

4. Cited in Fedigan, Linda Marie, 1982. *Primate Paradigms*, Eden Press, Montreal, p. 275.

5. Austad, Steven, 1990. "Individual Variation in Sperm Precedence," AAAS Annual Meeting Abstracts, Washington, D.C., p. 23.

6. Gould, James L., and Gould, Carol Grant, 1989. *Sexual Selection*, Scientific American Library, New York, p. 268.

7. Symons, D., 1979. *The Evolution of Human Sexuality*, Oxford University Press, New York, cited in Smith, Robert (ed.), "Human Sperm Competition," in *Sperm Competition and the Evolution of Animal Mating Systems*, 1984, Academic Press, Orlando, Florida, p. 634.

8. Smith, Robert, 1984. "Human Sperm Competition," in *Sperm Competition and the Evolution of Animal Mating Systems*, Robert Smith (ed.), Academic Press, Orlando, Florida, p. 634.

9. Smith, Robert, 1984. "Human Sperm Competition," pp. 633–34.

10. Ghileri, Michael Patrick, 1988. *East of the Mountains of the Moon: Chimpanzee Society in the African Jungle*, Free Press, New York.

11. Parker, G. A., 1984. "Sperm Competition and the Evolution of Animal Mating Strategies," in *Sperm Competition and the Evolution of Animal Mating Systems*, Robert Smith (ed.), Academic Press, Orlando, Florida, pp. 19–21.

12. Parker, G. A., 1990. "Sperm Competition Games," 1990 AAAS Annual Meeting Abstracts (compiled by Michelle D. Eames), AAAS Publications, Washington, D.C., p. 23.

13. Charles Darwin quote from *Sexual Selection and the Descent of*

Man, cited in Calvin, William, *Science,* June 24, 1988, p. 1803; for more on the misunderstandings concerning what an individual consists of within modern neo-Darwinian biology see Sagan, Dorion, "What Narcissus Saw: The Oceanic 'I,' " in *Speculations, The Reality Club,* Number 1, John Brockman (ed.), 1990, Prentice-Hall Press, New York, pp. 247–266.

2. Orgasm Equality

EPIGRAPH: Mead, Margaret, cited in Symons, D., 1979. *The Evolution of Human Sexuality,* Oxford University Press, New York, p. 90. Haraway, Donna, 1989. *Primate Visions,* Routledge, New York, p. 363.

1. Freud, cited in Gould, Stephen Jay, February, 1987. "Freudian Slip," *Natural History,* p. 18.

2. *Ibid.,* p. 15.

3. Kinsey, cited in Gould. *Ibid.,* p. 20.

4. Bolin, Anne, 1990. "The Transition from Physical Sexuality to Gender: A Cultural Process." 1990 AAAS Annual Meeting Abstracts, Washington, D.C., p. 121.

5. Peschel, Eenid Rhodes, and Peschel, Richard E., November-December, 1987. "Medical Insights into the Castrati in Opera," *American Scientist,* p. 579.

6. Casanova, J., 1961. *The Memoirs of Jacques Casanova de Seingalt,* (A. Machen, trans.), vol. 2, Dover, New York, p. 1303.

7. A further "mystery" of the human nipples concerns the areolae, the pink or brown pigmented patches surrounding the nipples themselves. The areolae have never been satisfactorily explained from an evolutionary point of view. Other primates—males and females—do not have these circular expanses around the nipples. One way humans differ from other primates is that, since we stand upright we naturally display what was earlier in evolution our hidden, belly side. Zoologist Desmond Morris—inspired by a Magritte painting of a woman whose eyes are breasts—wonders whether these patches surrounding the nipples, the areolae, might not look like the big eyes of an oncoming animal to another animal observing the human trunk from a distance. Moths are known to frighten off predators by opening their wings to display eye-spots that mimic the face of a much larger animal. Perhaps the large nipples of the human underside sometimes acted likewise. In Chapter 3 we will see how the human body constitutes a semiotic system, a network of signs, many of them sexual, that lead and mislead the members of both sexes.

8. Shulman quote, cited in Hite, 1976. *The Hite Report,* Macmillan, New York; recited in Wilson, Glen, *The Coolidge Effect: An Evolutionary Account of Human Sexuality,* 1982, William Morrow & Co., New York, p. 174.

9. Kinsey, cited in Symons, D., 1979. *The Evolution of Human Sexuality,* Oxford University Press, New York, pp. 82–83.

10. Haraway. *Primate Visions,* p. 356.

11. *Ibid.,* p. 358.

12. *Ibid.*, p. 356.

13. *Ibid.*, p. 357.

14. Lacan, cited in Benvenuto, Bice, and Kennedy, Roger, 1986. *The Works of Jacques Lacan, An Introduction*, St. Martin's Press, New York, p. 189.

15. Laqueur, Thomas, 1990. *Making Sex: Body and Gender from the Greeks to Freud*, Harvard University Press, Cambridge, Massachusetts. Laqueur believes that culturally developed models underlie and are in a deep sense impervious to the accumulation of scientific data. For many following in the tradition of French historian Michel Foucault, biology itself is a social construct, so that what we are tempted to think of as biological truths are in fact the product of historical contingency.

16. Cited in Gould. "Freudian Slip," p. 17.

17. Alcock, John, April, 1987. "Ardent Adaptationism," letter in *Natural History*, p. 4.

18. Wilson. *The Coolidge Effect*, p. 171.

19. Gould. "Freudian Slip," p. 18.

20. Hrdy, Sarah Blaffer, cited in Gould. "Freudian Slip," p. 18.

21. Fox, C. A., Wolff, H. S., and Baker, J. A., 1970. "Measurement of Intravaginal and Intra-uterine Pressures During Human Coitus by Radio Telemetry," *Journal of Reproductive Fertilization* 22: 243–51; Fox, C. A., and Fox, B., 1971. "A Comparative Study of Coital Physiology, with Special Reference to the Sexual Climax," *Journal of Reproductive Fertilization* 24: 319–36.

22. Cited in Smith. "Human Sperm Competition," p. 643.

23. *Ibid.*, p. 644.

24. Cited in Symons, D., 1979. *The Evolution of Human Sexuality*, Oxford University Press, New York, p. 93.

25. *Ibid.*

26. Leeuwenhoek's and ancient Indo-European remarks, cited in *The Importance of Feminist Critique for Modern Biology*, The Biology and Gender Study Group, Swarthmore, Pennsylvania. Unrevised version.

27. *Ibid.*

3. Body Electrick

EPIGRAPHS: Whitman, Walt, "I Sing the Body Electric." Stevens, Wallace, cited in Beilenson, Evelyn L., and Melnick, Sharon (eds.), 1987. *Words on Women, Quotes by Famous Americans*, Peter Pauper Press, White Plains, New York. Derrida, Jacques, 1976. *Of Grammatology* (Gayatri Chakravorty Spivak, trans.), John Hopkins University Press, Baltimore.

1. Cited in Allison, David (ed.), 1985. *The New Nietzsche, Contemporary Styles of Interpretation*, MIT Press, Cambridge, Massachusetts, pp. 159, 171.
As we saw before, gynophobia and mysogyny—fear of and distrustful anger toward women—may be rooted in the nearly universal practice of women not only bearing but rearing children. It is significant in this

context that Nietzsche was raised by his mother and her sisters, his father having died in a traumatic accident when Nietzsche was a boy.

2. Hrdy, Sarah Blaffer, 1977. *The Langurs of Abu, Female and Male Strategies of Reproduction*, Harvard University Press, Cambridge, Massachusetts.

3. Stoddart, D. Michael, 1990. *The Scented Ape: The Biology and Culture of Human Odour*. Cambridge University Press, Cambridge, England.

4. Fisher, Helen E., 1983. *The Sex Contract, The Evolution of Human Behavior*, Quill, New York, p. 144. Although female choice of male features is not the best explanation for the relatively large size of human penises, other male features, including some very irksome to women, may indeed be the result of female choice. The primatologist Irven DeVore has described men as a "vast breeding experiment run by females." When a female journalist with feminist leanings asked DeVore when men would become less macho and offensive, DeVore replied, "When women like you stop selecting high-success, strutting males like me." If one accepts the Darwinian notion of female choice, then it becomes clear that part of the dilemma of female attitudes toward men is that even the most undesirable traits, such as male chauvinism, are in part the result of former breeding choices by women. Female discussions of what traits are attractive in a man are not idle chatter but represent a serious meditation on the future direction of the male half of our species.

5. Forsyth, Adrian, 1986. *A Natural History of Sex, The Ecology and Evolution of Sexual Behavior*, Charles Scribner's Sons, New York, p. 35.

6. Cited in Morgan, Elaine, 1972. *The Descent of Woman*, Stein & Day, New York, p. 11.

7. *Ibid.*

8. Morris, Desmond, 1977. *Manwatching, A Field Guide to Human Behavior*, Harry N. Abrams, New York, p. 236.

9. Smith, Robert (ed.), 1984. "Human Sperm Competition," in *Sperm Competition and the Evolution of Animal Mating Systems*, Academic Press, Orlando, Florida, p. 641. (For alternative theories on the "loss of estrus" see, for example, Daly, Martin, and Wilson, Margo, 1983. *Sex, Evolution, and Behavior*, 2nd edition, PWS Publishers, Boston.)

10. *Ibid.*, p. 653.

11. MacLean, Paul D., 1976. "The Imitative-Creative Interplay of Our Three Mentalities," in *Astride the Two Cultures, Arthur Koestler at 70*, Harold Harris (ed.), Random House, New York; and see, MacLean, P. D., "The Brain's Generation Gap: Some Human Implications," *Zygon J. Relig. Sci.*, 1973, 8: 113–27.

12. Hrdy, Sarah Blaffer, 1986. "Empathy, Polyandry, and the Myth of the Coy Female," in *Feminist Approaches to Science*, Bleier, Ruth (ed.), Pergamon Press, New York, p. 152.

13. Wilson. *The Coolidge Effect*, pp. 149–50; 188–91.

14. Smith. "Human Sperm Competition," p. 642.

15. Forsyth. *A Natural History of Sex*, p. 96.

16. Smith. "Human Sperm Competition," p. 608.

17. Nobles, Edward, Autumn, 1988. The poem "Transmigrations of the

Innocent" can be found in *Yellow Silk: journal of the erotic arts*, No. 27, p. 7.

18. Fedigan, Linda Marie, 1982. *Primate Paradigms*, Eden Press, Montreal, p. 277.

4. Lizard Twists

EPIGRAPH: Butler, Samuel (1835–1902) uniquely conceived unconscious processes; ironically enough, we have not been able to relocate this quote (although it sounds like something from his Note-Books). A contemporary and would-be intellectual rival of Charles Darwin, Butler worked out a whole theory of the unconscious, publishing several books on the subject, long before Freud. In brief, for Butler, all the unconscious processes of an organism—for example, peristalsis, heartbeat, fetal growth—were at one time conscious. But they are so evolutionarily old, we have learned them so well, that they have become automatic, unconscious—just as, during the course of an individual lifetime, speaking, riding a skateboard, and driving a car can become "learned by heart" and therefore forgotten. Butler's phylogenetic memory is part of all living things, which set goals for themselves and then practice to unconscious perfection the means to achieve those goals. For Butler, the border between humanity and animality is still policed despite Charles Darwin's supposed breakthroughs. Butler would never agree to the distinction between natural selection (applied to all organisms) and cultural evolution (reserved for human beings) now common to evolutionary discourse.

2. Crews, David, December, 1987. "Courtship in Unisexual Lizards: A Model for Brain Evolution," *Scientific American*, 255: 12: 116–22.

3. *Ibid*.

4. Le Guin, Ursula K., 1969. *The Left Hand of Darkness*, Walker and Co., New York.

5. Percy, Walker, 1977. *Lancelot*, Farrar, Strauss, & Giroux, New York.

6. Maddox, Tom, 1988. "Snake-Eyes," in *Mirrorshades, The Cyberpunk Anthology*, Bruce Sterling (ed.), Ace Books, New York, p. 33.

7. Rothschild, Miriam, 1983. *Dear Lord Rothschild: Birds, Butterflies, and History*, Balaban Publishers, distributed by ISI Press, Philadelphia, pp. 68, 202–3, 315.

8. Greenberg, Neil, and MacLean, Paul D. (eds.), 1978. *Behavior and Neurology of Lizards*, National Institute of Mental Health, Bethesda, Maryland, p. 292.

9. Catton, Chris, and Gray, James, 1985. *Sex in Nature*, Facts on File Publications, New York, Oxford, p. 217.

10. Singer, June, 1977. *Androgyny: Toward a New Theory of Sexuality*, Anchor Books, Garden City, New York, pp. 172–73.

11. Kaufman, Walter, 1980. *Discovering the Mind: Freud versus Adler and Jung*, Vol. III, McGraw-Hill Book Company, p. 467.

12. Jerison, H. J., 1985. "Issues in Brain Evolution," in *Oxford Surveys in Evolutionary Biology*, Vol. II, Dawkins, R., and Ridley, M. (eds.), National Institute of Mental Health, Bethesda, Maryland, p. 128.

13. Jerison, H., 1973. *Evolution of the Brain and Intelligence*, Academic Press, New York, p. 17.

14. Jacob, François, 1982. *The Possible and the Actual*, Pantheon Books, New York, p. 57.

15. Jerison. *The Evolution of the Brain*, p. 19.

16. *Ibid.*, p. 20.

17. *Ibid.*, p. 23.

18. *Ibid.*, p. 427.

19. *Ibid.*, p. 23.

20. Calvin, W., 1990. *The Cerebral Symphony*, Bantam Books, New York.

21. Arber, Agnes, 1964. *The Mind and the Eye*, Cambridge University Press, Cambridge. pp. 4–5.

22. Arber. *The Mind and the Eye*, pp. 44–46.

23. Medawar, Peter, 1984. *Pluto's Republic*, Oxford University Press, New York, p. 254.

24. *Ibid.*, p. 72.

25. Cited in Allison, David (ed.), 1985. *The New Nietzsche, Contemporary Styles of Interpretation*, MIT Press, Cambridge, Massachusetts, p. 170.

26. Derrida, Jacques, 1978 (1967). "Freud and the Scene of Writing," in *Writing and Difference* (Alan Bass, trans.), University of Chicago Press, Chicago. p. 208.

27. *Ibid.*, p. 209.

28. Cited in *Ibid.*, p. 209.

29. MacLean, Paul D., 1978. "Why Brain Research on Lizards?," in *Behavior and Neurology of Lizards* (N. Greenberg and P.D. MacLean, eds.), National Institute of Mental Health, Bethesda, Maryland, p. 6.

30. *Ibid.*

31. Cited in Derrida, Jacques, 1978 (1967). "The Theater of Cruelty and the Closure of Representation," in *Writing and Difference* (Alan Bass, trans.), University of Chicago Press, Chicago, p. 239.

32. *Ibid.*, p. 241; although Freud is often taken to task by poststructuralists for his "biologisms," it is clear that the biological acts as a pillar without which the edifice of Freudian thought could never have been built in the first place. In the following passage from *The Ego and the Id*—the I and the it—we see graphically how close Freud comes to some of the claims being made here: "Thinking in pictures is, therefore, only a very incomplete form of becoming conscious. In some way, too, it stands nearer to unconscious processes than does thinking in words, and it is unquestionably older than the latter both ontogenetically and phylogenetically." Freud, Sigmund, 1960 (1923). *The Ego and the Id* (Joan Riviere, trans.); James Strachey (ed.), W. H. Norton and Co., New York.

33. *Ibid.*, p. 241.

5. Phallic Psyche

EPIGRAPHS: Smith, Patti quote from the album *Horses*; Rose, Jacqueline, 1982. "Introduction," in *Feminine Sexuality: Jacques Lacan and the école freudienne*, Rose, Jacqueline, and Mitchell, Juliet (eds.), W. H. Norton and Co., New York, p. 47.

1. Cited in Gallop, Jane, 1985. *Reading Lacan*, Cornell University Press, Ithaca, p. 330.

2. Freud, S., 1963. *Sexuality and the Psychology of Love*, Philip Rieff (ed.), Collier Books, New York, p. 215.

3. Gallop. *Reading Lacan*, p. 156.

4. The campaign to crucify pseudoscience in all its forms, the avowed claim of the Committee for the Scientific Investigation of Claims of the Paranormal (the CSICP and its literary outlet, *The Skeptical Inquirer*) is doomed to failure insofar as its members adopt the stance of righteous knights encharged with protection of the beleaguered citadel of science. Certainly we dwell in a historical time notable for the proliferation of belief systems dubious in the extreme, from New Age therapies to UFO religions. But the most dangerous forms of dubious thought have always been those that are most widely believed and institutionally protected. Such is the case with "science" insofar as that abstract noun represents an exact mode of inquiry or stable technique of practice. In fact, the unphilosophical acceptance of the assumption that science is a known, stable entity capable of being protected by a select few is as much a symptom of the present climate of nebulous beliefs and uncritical thinking as it is a potential cure.

5. Lacan, Jacques, 1977. *Écrits: A selection* (Alan Sheridan, trans.), W. H. Norton and Co., New York, pp. 282, 285, 288; cited in Gallop, p. 21.

6. Jacob, François, 1982. *The Possible and the Actual*, Pantheon Books, New York, p. 42. (Writing in *Le Monde*, Michel Foucault called this slim book (72 pages) "the most remarkable history of biology that has ever been written.")

7. Lacan. *Écrits: A selection*, p. 4.

8. Gallop. *Reading Lacan*, p. 80; Gallop's discussion of discovering the ironic lack of an original published work on the mirror stage is chronicled on pp. 74–92 of *Reading Lacan*, in the chapter entitled "Where to Begin?"

9. Lacan, Jacques, 1988. *The Seminar of Jacques Lacan*, Book 1, Freud's Papers on Techniques 1953–1954, Jacques-Alain Miller (ed.); (John Forrester, trans.), W. H. Norton and Co., New York, p. 73.

10. McCarthy, Barry, 1975. *Sexual Awareness, A Practical Approach*, Boyd and Fraser Publishing Co., San Francisco.

11. Parker, G. A., 1984. "Sperm Competition and the Evolution of Animal Mating Strategies," in *Sperm Competition and the Evolution of Animal Mating Systems*, Robert Smith (ed.), Academic Press, Orlando, Florida, p. 14.

12. Lacan. *The Seminar of Jacques Lacan*, p. 74.

13. Vanggaard, Thorkil, 1972. *Phallos, A Symbol and its History in the Male World* (translated from the Danish by the author), International Universities Press, New York, pp. 59–70.

14. Darwin, Charles, November 2, 1876. "Supplemental Note on Sexual Selection in Relation to Monkeys," *Nature*, pp. 921–24.

15. But it is also, as exemplified in Bataille's 1927 essay, "The Solar Anus," considerably more. If humans rise in evolution like a phallus, so

the object of this earthly erection is not a vaginal sky but—far more perversely—a solar anus. *"The solar annulus* is the intact anus of her body at eighteen years to which nothing sufficiently blinding can be compared except the sun, even though the *anus* is the *night."* (Bataille, Georges, 1985. *Visions of Excess, Selected Writings,* 1927–1939, Allan Stoekl (ed.); [Allan Stoekl, Carl R. Lovitt, and Donald M. Leslie, Jr., trans.], University of Minnesota Press, Minneapolis, p. 9.)

By rigorously associating the sun neither with the head or the king but with the anus, Bataille accomplishes a powerful reversal of a conceptual hierarchy we have inherited—whether we realized it or not—from medieval times. Sexualizing the universe ("The sea continuously jerks off" *Ibid.* p. 8), and using the language of rationality to parody logical explanatory discourse, Bataille in this essay is one of the first to practice both deconstruction and postmodernism.

6. Subvisible Survivors

EPIGRAPH: Shelley, Percy Bysshe, *Poems and Lyrics.*

1. Robson, Simon, 1987. "Book Review" (of Margulis, Lynn, and Sagan, Dorion, 1986. *The Origins of Sex: Three Billion Years of Genetic Recombination,* Yale University Press, New Haven). *Symbiosis,* 3: 207–12, Balaban Publishers, Philadelphia/Rehovot, p. 211.

2. Gould, Stephen Jay, 1986. "Evolution and the Triumph of Homology, or Why History Matters," *American Scientist,* 74: 60–69.

3. Cleveland, Lemuel R., 1949. "The Origin and Evolution of Meiosis," *Science,* vol. 105, pp. 287–88.

4. The arcane tale of sex in the Proterozoic Eon (2500–580 million years ago) and the relation of sex to the beginning of animals is detailed in Margulis and Sagan, 1986. *Origins of Sex,* Yale University Press, New Haven.

5. Cited in Weber, Samuel, 1982. *The Legend of Freud,* p. 158, University of Minnesota Press, Minneapolis.

6. Cited in *Ibid.,* p. 159.

7. Cherfas, Jeremy, and Gribbin, John, 1984. *The Redundant Male: Is Sex Irrelevant in the Modern World?,* Pantheon Books, New York; Hapgood, Fred, *Why Males Exist: An Inquiry into the Evolution of Sex,* 1979, William Morrow & Co., New York; Maranto, Gina, and Brownlee, Shannon, February, 1984. "Why Sex?", *Discover,* pp. 24–28.

8. See Trivers, Robert, 1985. *Social Evolution,* Benjamin/Cummings Publishing Company, pp. 315–30 for a good overview of the maintenance of sex "problem" from a Darwinian perspective; further details concerning the theoretical contributions of the main players in this discussion can be found in the popular accounts listed in the preceding reference.

9. Dobzhansky, Theodosius, 1973. "Nothing in biology makes sense except in the light of evolution." *American Biology Teacher* 35: 125–29.

Index